The Pensions Book

The Pensions Book

A practical guide for the busy company secretary

Michael Harvey

Chief Executive
Buck Consultants

ICSA Publishing
The Official Publishing Company of
The Institute of Chartered Secretaries and Administrators

First published 1996 by
ICSA Publishing Limited
Campus 400, Maylands Avenue
Hemel Hempstead
Hertfordshire, HP2 7EZ

Typeset in 10/12pt Palatino
by PPS, London Road, Amesbury, Wilts.

Printed and bound in Great Britain by
T. J. Press (Padstow) Ltd

British Library Cataloguing in Publication Data

A catalogue record for this book is available from
the British Library

ISBN 1-87286069-9 (pbk)

1 2 3 4 5   00 99 98 97 96

Contents

Preface   ix

1   Introduction   1

A Opening Pandora's box   3

2   Types of pension scheme   5
   2.1 Defined contribution or defined benefit?   5
   2.2 Insured pension schemes   7
   2.3 Self-administered pension schemes   10
   2.4 Insured versus self-administered   11
   2.5 Additional voluntary contributions (AVCs)   12
   2.6 Individual arrangements   13
   2.7 Personal pension arrangements   14
   2.8 Contracting-out   16
   2.9 Unapproved schemes   17

B Identifying your needs   19

3   Choosing your advisers   21
   3.1 Pensions consultancy   22
   3.2 The actuary   27
   3.3 Investment consultant   28
   3.4 The legal adviser   29
   3.5 Auditors   30
   3.6 Investment managers   30
   3.7 Advisers: to whom?   32
   3.8 Scheme administrator   32
   3.9 Trustees   34
4   Designing the scheme   39
   4.1 Initial considerations   39
   4.2 The defined benefit scheme   41
   4.3 The defined contribution scheme   51
   4.4 Flexible benefits   52
   4.5 Conclusion   52

5   Balance of powers   54
    5.1 Taking decisions   54
    5.2 Parties and powers   56
    5.3 Getting the balance right   64
    5.4 Conclusion   65

C The scheme in operation   67

6   Day-to-day administration   69
    6.1 Contributions   69
    6.2 Benefits   70
    6.3 Record-keeping   76
    6.4 Communication   81

7   Investment matters   88
    7.1 Investment powers   89
    7.2 Investment strategy   89
    7.3 Investment risk   91
    7.4 Liability profile of the scheme   92
    7.5 Investment vehicle   93
    7.6 Investment manager structure   93
    7.7 Manager selection   95
    7.8 Monitoring of manager performance   96

8   Security and protection of members' interests   99
    8.1 Insurance policies and pooled funds   99
    8.2 Self-administered schemes   100
    8.3 Remedies available to beneficiaries   106

9   Paying for the benefits   109
    9.1 The actuary's role   109
    9.2 Defined contribution schemes   111
    9.3 The actuarial valuation   111
    9.4 Surplus   115
    9.5 Transfer values   117
    9.6 Other considerations   118

10 Audit and review   121
    10.1 Scheme benefit structure   122
    10.2 General administration   124
    10.3 Conclusion   126

D Current topics and future implications   127

11   The earnings cap   129
      11.1 What is the earnings cap?   129
      11.2 Unapproved retirement benefits schemes   131
      11.3 Unfunded unapproved retirement benefits schemes
          (UURBS)   132
      11.4 Funded unapproved retirement benefits schemes (FURBS)   137
      11.5 Retirement planning using unapproved schemes   141

12   Live issues   143
      12.1 Equality between the sexes   143
      12.2 Inflation-proofing   148
      12.3 The Maxwell affair   150
      12.4 The Goode recommendations   151
      12.5 The White Paper   154
      12.6 The 1995 Pensions Act   156
      12.7 Pension rights on divorce   157
      12.8 The Government's agenda   157
      12.9 Conclusion   161

Glossary of terms   162

Appendix 1 State pension schemes and contracting-out   188

Appendix 2 Inland Revenue limits for tax-approved schemes   190

Index   194

Preface

In accepting an invitation to present a paper on 'Key issues concerning the governance of pension plans' to the Company Secretaries' Conference 1993, I little realised the future implications! Some members in the audience were keen to expand their knowledge in this area – but from the viewpoint of the Company Secretary's role in helping the Board of Directors to understand the impact the pension scheme has on the company and its employees, the dos and don'ts in pensions and attempting to get good practical advice in a cost-effective way.

The discussions clearly went well and I was subsequently asked to consider writing a book on pensions. Having read many I thought this could be my Waterloo! However, having accepted the challenge I benefited considerably from the contributions of several of my colleagues and I would like to thank them all for their suggestions and comments.

Kevin LeGrand in particular has played a key role in the structuring, drafting and technical comment and we are now both so familiar with the book that we are able to offer recitals on request!

Carole Pudney, who has typed the various drafts, has been severely tested and passed with flying colours. Despite her diplomatic attempts to improve my handwriting I continue to make too infrequent use of the pencil sharpeners!

Antony Tuffin and Peter Armitage gave very valuable constructive comment when reviewing the drafts before going to press. At the time of writing we have seen the completion of the passage of the 1995 Pensions Bill through Parliament which, together with changes in European law, suggests that a second edition will soon need to be considered.

Michael Harvey
Buck Consultants
London
July 1995

1 Introduction

Pension schemes are an enigma in today's social, economic and business worlds. They have far-reaching effects in each of these areas and yet they are barely understood by those who benefit directly from them. Their running is often delegated by companies to those who draw the shortest straws, assisted by highly remunerated professionals who are often given *carte blanche* to instigate changes when they feel them to be necessary.

This attitude is surprising when one considers the financial implications of pension schemes. To the members, their pensions may well represent their biggest asset (often worth more than the houses in which they live). To the company it may be just a necessary evil, but one which could swallow annual contributions of between 10 per cent and 15 per cent of payroll. The finance director frequently complains about the cost, but how closely is the running of the scheme actually monitored by company management? Is the company really getting value for the assets tied up in the scheme? After all, to the company the scheme is simply a business tool and should earn its keep, like any other.

However, pension schemes are very complicated. The law governing them is a stew of trusts, taxation, employment and social security law, with a touch of contract law thrown in to taste. Add to that details of fund investment and actuarial complexities and to many it is a recipe for certain indigestion. From a personal point of view, members (whether management or other employees) similarly are rarely motivated to get to grips with the complexities of the subject until retirement is staring them in the face, because to do so earlier would be to admit the unpleasant truth that if we live long enough, we will grow old.

Looked at in this light it is therefore not surprising that occupational pension schemes remain a mystery which few understand and are able to control. However, given the costs involved, and the fact that demographic changes and other pressures on the public purse are persuading the Government to shift an ever greater part of the pensions burden onto the private sector, it is an area which companies continue to ignore at their peril.

The management representative to whom the job of watching over the pension scheme is frequently devolved is the company secretary (possibly with the additional responsibility of being a trustee). Given the company secretary's other duties, it is virtually impossible for him or her to find

1

enough time to exercise effective control. In the time available, he or she can often do little other than consider superficially the various pieces of paper sent by the professionals running the scheme. Yet he or she must control the people who are actually running the scheme.

The purpose of this book is to assist the busy company secretary in doing just that – as a company representative, not as a trustee. It aims to be a practical friend, giving sufficient information to enable readers to understand what should be happening, without deluging them with unnecessary detail and jargon. Using this as a guide, readers should be able to ask the right questions of the professionals, and assess the suitability of the answers received. They should be able to identify the situations in which they will need to have a more detailed involvement, and when they or management colleagues will be called upon to take a decision. The book also points out some of the more common pitfalls which lay in wait to trap the unwary.

By progressing through a series of related chapters, readers will consider all the main areas of concern to companies running occupational pension schemes. The final chapter examines those issues that are currently causing problems for schemes, and speculates on what is to come.

The future itself is an area to which some thought should be given now. Following the Maxwell scandal, the Government appointed the Pensions Law Review Committee under Professor Roy Goode to look into the whole area of law governing pension schemes and to recommend changes where necessary. The Committee reported at the end of September 1993, making 218 specific recommendations. The Government subsequently issued the White Paper on 'Security, equality, choice: the future for pensions' with the aim of achieving 'the greatest practicable security in all schemes without imposing unnecessary burdens on those that are well run.' The majority of recommendations in the Goode Report have been accepted in full or in part and have led to a Pensions Act during the 1994/95 parliamentary session.

These two documents have stimulated wide-ranging and detailed discussions on almost every aspect of the law and good practice in respect of occupational pensions. The full details of prospective legislation are still being considered. However, all those with an interest in running a company pension scheme would do well to obtain, and then keep up to date, an overview of the situation.

Coping with the new legislation when it happens will require considerable expert help. This book will be an invaluable aid to that process.

A Opening Pandora's box

This section introduces the different types of pension scheme. It aims to give an understanding of the different classifications of schemes and of some of the jargon.

2 Types of pension scheme

Pension schemes can be categorised in a number of different ways, but it is important to understand the variations available, before going on to consider the most appropriate design for your scheme. Schemes may involve these features in various combinations, and that aspect is dealt with in Chapter 4. To gain tax approval all pension arrangements have to satisfy certain conditions concerning the way they are established, their day-to-day operation and the maximum contributions and benefits which are allowed. Those aspects have been included in Appendix 2.

2.1 Defined contribution or defined benefit?

This is a fundamental question affecting both the form of the benefits being provided and, perhaps more importantly, where the main responsibility for the cost of those benefits will lie.

2.1.1 Defined contribution

These schemes are often referred to as 'money purchase'. The underlying concept is that the contributions paid to the scheme (whether by the employer or employee) are defined either as a percentage of some definition of the member's remuneration or as a level amount. The contributions are then invested by the trustees and each member's benefit from the scheme is the value of the contributions paid in his or her name, increased (or decreased) by the investment return on them. At the point of retirement or death (if earlier) this sum is used to secure an annuity, with (on retirement) the possibility of taking at least some of the fund as a tax-free cash sum. Clearly, in such an arrangement the member bears the investment risk and has no guarantee of the final pension at retirement. The company has a fixed controllable cost.

2.1.2 Defined benefit

The underlying principle is that the benefit which will be provided to the member from the scheme is the element which is guaranteed. This either may be expressed as a proportion of a defined part of a member's remuneration over his or her career with the company or at or near the date of retirement or death, or may be expressed as a fixed sum for each year of service spent in a particular remuneration grade or band. If the benefit is based on remuneration at or near retirement, the scheme is usually known as 'final salary'. The member may or may not be required to contribute, but if he or she is so required, such a contribution may be expressed as some proportion of his or her remuneration or alternatively as a specified sum. In a few schemes the employer's and employee's contributions may be in a fixed ratio so that if the employer's contribution increases so does that of the employee.

Since the benefit is effectively guaranteed, and the investment return on the fund held by the trustees to provide the benefits is naturally subject to the usual fluctuations in investment performance, it follows that the employer is the party left to pick up the balance of the cost required to fund the promised benefits. For this reason, such schemes are often also known as 'balance of cost' schemes.

Clearly this potentially open-ended cost liability gives the employer a significant interest in a number of aspects of the way in which the scheme is run – and especially in the investment performance of the funds under the trustees' control. This is the main reason why pension schemes are probably unique in trust law in giving the settlor (i.e. the employer) a considerable degree of ongoing influence in the scheme once it has been set up. This creates potential conflicts of interest with the trustees and requires very careful consideration of the balance between the powers held by the two parties – a subject considered in more detail in Chapter 5.

2.1.3 Hybrid schemes

It is possible to combine both of these concepts in a single scheme. The ways in which these can be done are dealt with in more detail in Chapter 4, but for the purposes of this chapter it is necessary only to know that a combination is possible, such as providing a guaranteed benefit calculated as a proportion of a member's remuneration at retirement, combined with a promise that if he or she leaves prior to reaching retirement age, he or she will be entitled to a benefit not less than that which can be purchased by a notional fund calculated by taking the member's and the employer's contributions on his or her behalf and applying a notional investment return on them. This device is quite commonly used to improve the attractiveness of company schemes to those who may leave early, and its uses are explored more fully in Chapter 4. These types of scheme are often known as 'hybrids', 'final salary with money purchase underpin', 'money purchase with final salary overlay' or possibly 'targeted money purchase'.

Regardless of how the assets are invested, or who is entrusted with the job of running the scheme, the benefits will be of one of these types. Schemes are, however, classified in other ways. Let us now look at some of these.

2.2 Insured pension schemes

Insured pension schemes use some form of grouped investment contract. They can be defined benefit or defined contribution arrangements for individuals or groups. The term covers such areas as the following:

1. Additional voluntary contributions (AVCs).
2. Free-standing additional voluntary contributions (FSAVCs).
3. Group personal pensions.
4. Individual pension arrangements.
5. Personal pensions (PPs).

Individual pension arrangements (which in various guises can be used as top-up arrangements over and above benefits provided from a group scheme) are often of a defined benefit nature but the other schemes are usually on a defined contribution basis. At retirement the annuity is expected to be secured with the life office issuing the original pension contract. However nowadays, with most defined contribution contracts and many defined benefit insured schemes, it is possible to go to the market and purchase the pension annuity at retirement from another life office if more competitive terms are then available. Such a facility is known as an 'open market option'.

Essentially in an insured scheme the benefits under the scheme are matched exactly by one or more insurance policies written specifically for the scheme. As such, insured schemes are ideally suited to small companies requiring security and guarantees. The insurance company is involved in the scheme investments and in practice will also cover most of the additional services related to pension schemes, such as administration, actuarial, documentation, accounts, benefit statements and other communication material, such as the member's booklet.

Where an employer has opted for a group insured scheme there will usually be three investment options to choose from in order to provide the benefits outlined in the scheme documentation. These are normally a with-profit deferred annuity contract, a deposit administration contract or a unitised fund.

2.2.1 With-profit deferred annuities

A deferred annuity is simply an annuity which commences from a future date. When first introduced, the basis on which these could be purchased was non-profit whereby in exchange for a fixed and defined premium, a fixed and defined amount of pension was provided. These schemes were commonly classed as 'graded schedule' schemes whereby members whose salary fell into a particular grade were entitled to a specified amount of pension for each year of service. For example:

salary grade

A = salaries £3,000 – £3,499: pension for each year of service = £30

B = salaries £3,500 – £3,999: pension for each year of service = £35

C = salaries £4,000 – £4,499: pension for each year of service = £40

and so on.

In the early 1960s it was recognised that a group contract offering an investment yield of between 4 and 6 per cent per annum was beginning to prove unattractive in the changing investment climate of those times. Consequently the life offices began to offer contracts which provided for life, from a defined age, a guaranteed amount of pension (although initially lower than under a non-profit contract) and also carried the right to participate in the profits of that particular life office. Profits are declared in the form of bonuses which once added cannot be removed. This produces a more stable return than that from direct investment and reflects the insurance element of the contract. Whereas the underlying investment return was perhaps only $3–3\frac{1}{2}$ per cent, there was the probability of a very much higher yield from bonuses, although perhaps less than would have been earned by direct investment. Such yields have fluctuated in recent years from highs of $14\frac{1}{2}$–15 per cent to the 8–10 per cent which was available in 1994. Even so, such yields give considerable added value to those that were available under the original non-profit deferred annuity contracts.

2.2.2 Deposit administration

Here contributions, net of expenses and charges, are accumulated in a pool to which interest and/or bonuses are added and cannot subsequently be removed. The rate of interest is variable and tends to reflect market interest rates on a year-to-year basis. Separate tranches of contributions within the pool can be identified and consequently attract differing rates of interest. The contract in many ways operates in a similar way to a normal building society deposit account.

As employees retire, monies are released from the pool in order to purchase annuities. Unlike deferred annuities, premiums are being placed on deposit and not exchanged for benefits on the basis of a premium rate table.

2.2.3 Unitised funds

Contributions, again net of expenses and charges, are used to purchase units in a pooled fund, investing directly in stocks and shares. The price of units rises and falls in line with movements in the underlying stocks and shares. Whether the insurance contract is for an individual or a group, the documentation, administration, and all other functions associated with running the arrangement are provided by the insurance company.

There is a variety of different unitised funds in which to invest, from specialist funds such as small company funds or a Japanese fund to a mixed fund covering a range of different types of investment. Such a mixed fund is also known as a balanced fund or managed fund. However 'managed fund' is also a generic term used for any pooled investment vehicle.

Managed funds are identical in concept to a unit trust. The pool of investments is divided into a fixed number of units held initially by the insurance company or investment house. These units fall and rise in value in accordance with the performance of the underlying investments. As a pension scheme pays premiums or raises money for payment of benefits so it buys or sells units, which are similarly being bought and sold by other participating pension schemes. The value of the pension scheme's interest in the managed fund is therefore determined at any time by the number of units held by that scheme and the price of those units at that time. To cater for the varying requirements of trustees who now use managed funds, all fund managers have a range of funds specialising in equities (both UK and overseas), UK gilts (fixed and index-linked), property, small companies, cash, etc. There is also normally a mixed fund of some description, which itself invests in some or all of the other, specialised, funds, with a manager responsible for selecting the mix.

Managed funds are provided by insurance companies and investment houses alike. There is really no insurance element in a managed fund: unit prices fall and rise directly in line with the underlying investments. All other services associated with the running of the pension scheme are 'unbundled' and may be provided by a variety of different organisations.

The costs associated with managed funds investment are direct costs, i.e. fees charged by the fund manager, but apart from this the investment returns, both capital and income, belong to the participating pension scheme as unit holder, and are directly reflected in the unit price. For small to medium-sized pension schemes, with assets of less than £10m, their funds would usually form part of a much larger pool with similar sized funds.

When benefits become payable, monies can either be released from the managed fund, by the 'sale' of the appropriate number of units, or if the contribution input to the pension scheme is sufficiently large, the required sum of money can be provided from future contributions by diverting them away from the managed fund investment.

In order to retain monies in their own internal funds, holding insurance companies often offer enhanced annuity rates to their managed fund clients. The process of achieving this is by the insurance company offering annuity rates which can perhaps be up to 5 per cent better than those on the 'open' market at the time. This encourages the pension scheme to 'buy' the annuity with the insurance company, so that the purchase price of the annuity remains with the insurance company.

2.3 Self-administered pension schemes

Insured pension schemes are primarily, although not exclusively, more appropriate to the smaller employer with limited personal, corporate and associated systems resources. However, a managed fund can also form part of the investments of a self-administered pension scheme. This, broadly, is a scheme which is not tied to insurance contracts. In such a scheme the opportunity exists to arrange for all the component services (including investment) to be handled separately, possibly by different institutions. As an example the pension scheme administration may be handled internally (if the sponsoring employer is sufficiently large) whilst actuarial input will be provided by a firm of independent consultants. Documentation and legal services may be provided by a firm of specialist pension solicitors, whilst communication material will be produced with the assistance of communication specialists. This gives considerable extra flexibility to schemes, having broken with the insurance company 'package' approach, and allows freedom to organise the scheme on the basis most appropriate to the needs both of the members and the company, often with resultant cost savings.

The investment of scheme monies may be via unitised or managed funds or directly in stocks and shares, property, etc. when it is known as a segregated fund; this is covered in Chapter 7.

2.3.1 Small self-administered schemes (SSAS)

These are a variation of self-administered schemes. The denomination 'small' does not refer to the size of the funds under the trustees' control (indeed, these can be of significant amounts) but to the number of members. Normally, any self-administered scheme with fewer than twelve members will automatically be categorised as an SSAS. Such schemes are usually established to provide benefits for entrepreneurs who control their own small companies, or for small groups of senior executives seeking membership of a scheme which provides them with superior benefits which are not disclosable to other employees.

The SSAS concept has been in existence since 1973 when the Finance Act of that year first allowed controlling directors to become members of company pension schemes. (Prior to that time their only method of providing income in retirement had been by effecting 'retirement annuity policies with insurance companies' – see section 2.7) The great attraction to many entrepreneurs of such a scheme is the ability to invest (subject to a number of restrictions) up to 50 per cent of the scheme's funds, either directly or indirectly in the sponsoring company. A director of a small company can therefore put aside funds in a tax-efficient manner to provide for retirement income, still using a proportion of them to help fund the existing business.

Because of the small number of members of such schemes, the PSO (Pension Schemes Office of the Inland Revenue) is extremely worried about the potential abuse of the tax concessions granted, through misuse of funds held by the trustees. Consequently, these schemes are the most heavily regulated of all occupational schemes. As part of this process the PSO, uniquely, requires one of the trustees to be a pensions specialist, tagged the 'pensioneer trustee'. The pensioneer trustee's job is specifically to prevent the scheme being wound-up and the funds used for a purpose other than the provision of retirement benefits for the members. However, unofficially, the pensioneer trustee is frequently drawn into matters affecting the day-to-day running of the scheme (with the obvious effect on running costs). The running of such schemes is a specialist area and not considered in this book. Suffice it to say that a competent consultant will be able to steer an employer through the technical difficulties created by such schemes.

2.4 Insured versus self-administered

With insurance contracts, and managed funds (to a lesser extent), there are charges which are either built into the premium rates or allowed for in the return on the funds invested. With managed funds the charge usually takes the form of an annual management charge and a bid/offer spread, not normally exceeding 5 per cent on the price of the fund units. This is the difference between the buying and selling price of the units, the bid price (that at which the scheme buys the units) being higher than the offer, or selling, price. This difference is used to meet some of the management charges. Alternatively a flat rate charge instead can be levied on the pension scheme at the beginning of each year. Whereas the bid/offer cost directly affects the pension scheme to the extent that it buys or sells units, the flat rate charge ignores this and, as a consequence, a low activity scheme probably pays a higher proportionate cost than a very active scheme.

Self-administered schemes have charges which have to be met separately. These are often met directly by the sponsoring employer, but can be paid out of the fund and subsequently reflected in the future contribution rate for a defined benefit scheme. This will be of necessity because, as mentioned previously, several separate organisations may be involved in handling a self-administered scheme, all with separate charges. As a consequence, self-administered schemes are more likely to be appropriate for the larger employer who either has the resources to provide services in-house or sees an advantage in exercising greater control by retaining the flexibility to replace the provider of a service in the event of poor performance. This can be done without disrupting other aspects of the pension scheme. For insured schemes, changing to new insurers can be particularly difficult. Transferring membership data is always problematical and there can be significant communication and documentation issues to resolve. There can often be a penalty applied in cashing assets. Depending on the period that the assets had been held by the insurance company, this penalty could be reasonably severe, leaving perhaps only 60–70 per cent of the full value of the fund available at the date of disinvestment.

Whether the administration function is handled internally or passed to a third party it would not be unusual to find an internal pensions manager (part- or full-time) coordinating the various services for a self-administered scheme.

2.5 Additional voluntary contributions (AVCs)

Every employer-sponsored occupational pension scheme is obliged by law to offer an AVC facility to its members. This facility is for members themselves to make contributions to the scheme (in addition to any which they may be required under the scheme's rules to make) to fund extra benefits at retirement. Occupational schemes are governed by an Inland Revenue regime which specifies the maximum benefits which can be taken from the scheme. However, providing benefits at the maximum permitted by the Inland Revenue is extremely expensive and very few scheme members are granted such generous benefits. Consequently the AVC facility exists for members to fund part or all of the shortfall.

The AVC facility attached to a scheme involves the members' contributions being paid to the trustees and held under the same trust as the other assets of the pension scheme. However, funds resulting from AVCs must be separately identifiable, and so consequently are frequently placed in an investment medium different from that used to hold the funds for the balance of the scheme. The proceeds of AVCs are also commonly held in separate funds because, by their nature, they are being used to fund the benefits of particular individuals and so will be withdrawn at different times and frequencies from the assets constituting the main fund under the scheme.

This point also dictates the choice of investment medium for AVCs. Since one of the uses to which AVCs may be put is to fund the additional cost involved in a member retiring early and taking his or her pension immediately from an earlier date than he or she would otherwise have done, it is important for AVCs to be invested in suitable contracts which can take account of such needs and avoid early surrender penalties. The trustees are normally responsible for selecting the fund or funds into which AVCs may be paid, and so they must be careful to ensure that an appropriate investment vehicle is offered.

All the comments so far have assumed that AVCs will be applied to provide additional benefits on a 'money purchase' basis. This is the most common situation, regardless of whether the main scheme benefits are on the 'defined benefit', 'defined contribution' or other basis. Some schemes do offer fixed pension benefits in return for the payment of AVCs. However, as with all other defined benefits promised from schemes, the employer ultimately bears the risk of investment performance not meeting expectations, with the result that the company will end up underwriting the loss. AVC arrangements on this basis are relatively rare therefore in the private sector.

A further variation on the AVC theme was introduced in 1987 – the so-called 'free-standing additional voluntary contribution' (FSAVC) arrangement. This is an arrangement to which the member subscribes, and which provides benefits in return for member contributions outside the scheme. A member cannot subscribe to such a scheme without also being a member of an occupational pension scheme.

FSAVC schemes are run by approved providers such as insurance companies, banks and building societies. In many ways these contracts are akin to personal pension arrangements (see section 2.7). They provide benefits only on a 'money purchase' basis and are designed solely to augment benefits under the occupational pension scheme. The advantage to the adventurous members is that the market is large and the investment options almost limitless. However, the downside is that unlike AVC arrangements connected to the occupational scheme where the employer generally bears the administration costs and can call on his external investment advisers to monitor progress of the funds, a member with an FSAVC arrangement bears all the costs associated with the contract, and cannot generally expect the employer to provide any advice or other assistance.

Although trustees cannot prevent members from contributing to FSAVC arrangements they still have some responsibility for ensuring that the aggregate benefits from both the occupational scheme and the FSAVC arrangement do not exceed the appropriate benefit limits set out by the Inland Revenue. They therefore need to be as aware of the benefits emerging from this source as they would be of those arising from their in-scheme AVC facilities.

2.6 Individual arrangements

With the limited exception of FSAVC arrangements, all the types of schemes mentioned so far have been of the 'group' variety, that is, a single trust governing the benefits for a number of members. The scheme is designed to last in perpetuity if necessary (subject to any changes along the way which are deemed necessary to keep it relevant to the needs of members and the sponsoring company and the social and economic backgrounds applicable at the time) and members will therefore come and go, with the scheme remaining otherwise intact.

An alternative in the sphere of occupational pension provision is the 'individual arrangement'. This is, as its name suggests, an arrangement solely for the benefit of one individual, but it is nevertheless set up under a separate trust by the employer, with trustees being appointed, and being subject to the same Revenue regulatory regime as applies to 'group' schemes sponsored by the employer. These individual arrangements are usually established either to preserve the confidentiality of benefits being given to a senior employee, or to enable an employee who is an existing member of a group scheme to receive additional benefits funded by the employer – where again confidentiality is often the predominant factor.

Traditionally such arrangements are insured schemes purchased as a standard package from an insurance company. They may provide guaranteed pension benefits (albeit on a very conservative basis and through the use of a 'with-profits' policy) or may be set up on a money purchase basis, possibly targeted to provide a final salary type benefit. Although they give the advantage of individual flexibility and confidentiality, the downside is clearly a higher unit cost in running the arrangement because of a lack of opportunity to spread the running costs over a group of members.

2.7 Personal pension arrangements

The term 'personal pension' (PP) is now usually applied to an arrangement which is approved under Chapter IV of Part XIV of the Income and Corporation Taxes Act 1988, through which individuals who are self-employed or who are not members of an occupational pension scheme (they are in 'non-pensionable employment') may make pension provision on an individual basis. PPs are written in the names of individual policyholders. This means that, unlike occupational pension schemes, the PP arrangement itself travels with the individual member when he or she changes employment. This makes each PP potentially extremely versatile, being capable of taking contributions from the member, whether self-employed or employed by another, and also from any employer of the member. If the member, during his or her career, is at various times self-employed and employed by another, the same PP may continue as the chosen pension vehicle for the whole of that career. It is this 'portability' which makes the PP arrangement attractive to many people who anticipate changing their employment frequently during their career.

PP arrangements are written solely on a money purchase basis. They must be written by a pension provider approved by the Inland Revenue. Approved providers include banks, building societies, insurance companies, friendly societies and others. Each of these organisations will invest the PP monies in investment products which they themselves provide. In addition, it is now possible to obtain a 'self-administered PP'. This allows the member to select his or her own investment medium which is not an insurance contract or a unit trust, so enabling the entrepreneurial member to invest in such things as property connected with his or her business. The number of providers in the market is increasing but the restraints usually imposed under their contracts can be restrictive on the investment media and initial setting up costs can be high.

The rules governing both benefits and contributions for PPs differ greatly from those applicable to occupational schemes. In particular the maximum benefit which can be provided through a PP is limited only by the size of the fund accrued at the date of retirement, although the amount which can be taken as (tax-free) cash cannot exceed 25 per cent of this fund. Contributions are limited and are stepped according to age. Further details are contained in Appendix 2.

2.7.1 Appropriate personal pension arrangements

It is not possible to contribute to a PP whilst also accruing benefits under an occupational pension scheme, unless the PP is an appropriate personal pension (APP). A minimum or rebate only APP is used solely for contracting-out of the state earnings-related pension scheme (SERPS) and receives only the portion of the National Insurance (NI) contributions which are paid by and in respect of the member to the Department of Social Security (DSS) to cover the cost of SERPS participation and which are then rebated by the DSS to the APP provider.

PP arrangements are also commonly used as a home for transfer values from occupational schemes when members leave before normal retirement date, and have been the enabling vehicle for the pensions transfer scandal of the early 1990s.

2.7.2 Retirement annuity contracts

PPs replaced the old 'retirement annuity contracts' (RACs) which were previously available to the self-employed. These were not as flexible as PPs. The maximum contribution rate which could be paid to them was lower than those which can now be paid to PPs but contributions to RACs are not restricted by the 'earnings cap' introduced in 1989 (see Chapter 11) so it is sometimes possible to pay more to a RAC than a PP. Since the introduction of PPs in 1988, it has not been possible to commence a new RAC. However, many of them are still in existence and are at present allowed to continue receiving premiums. They can co-exist happily with PPs, although the contributions limit to the latter is reduced by the contributions being paid to the RAC.

2.7.3 Group personal pensions

A group personal pension 'scheme' is not a scheme in the legal sense, nor in the eyes of the Inland Revenue, but is a collection of individual personal pension arrangements arranged together for ease of employer adminis-tration. The employer will have arranged for the contracts of a limited number of providers to be made available to employees. The employer's involvement may also extend to providing technical information to em-ployees, collecting their contributions through the payroll system, and even to contributing itself. The employer can very often negotiate a reduction in administrative costs per contract by being able to arrange for a particular number of employees to join. A group PP therefore provides a useful means by which an employer may make pension arrangements available for its employees, but at minimal cost to itself.

Although a group PP scheme is not technically a 'scheme' in the legal or Inland Revenue sense, it does constitute a scheme for the purposes of the preservation regulations where the employer contributes to it. Great care must therefore be taken when designing such 'schemes' to ensure that the design does not leave the employer with an obligation under the preservation regulations to provide benefits on leaving in excess of those which will become available at that time under the individual PP contracts.

2.8 Contracting-out

There is an option for employed individuals who pay NI contributions at the full rate and have earnings above the lower earnings level (LEL) to contract out of SERPS. This can be achieved in one of two ways: firstly, by being a member of an occupational pension scheme, which will then provide at least a SERPS-equivalent element, or secondly, by commencing a PP arrangement when the appropriate NI contributions are re-directed to an approved provider's contract, so that these may be invested and produce a pension in place of SERPS.

Between 1978 (when SERPS was introduced) and 1988 (when personal pension arrangements first became available) it was only possible to contract out of SERPS through membership of an approved defined benefit pension scheme. The part of the benefit which replaced the SERPS pension forgone was also provided on a defined benefit basis and was called a guaranteed minimum pension (GMP). However, with the advent of the new, more liberal and flexible regime introduced from 1988, it became possible to contract out of SERPS through the provision of a money purchase benefit. It is this basis upon which a PP arrangement contracts out. The fund which is specifically allocated to the replacement of the SERPS pension foregone is known as the protected rights fund. This option to contract out on a money purchase basis is also now available to members of occupational schemes. This means that an occupational scheme may offer a contracting-out option to members on either a money purchase or defined benefit basis, regardless of the basis on which the underlying main benefits of the scheme are provided.

There is a fundamental difference between the way in which the protected rights fund is made up under an occupational scheme and a PP. In the former case the employer deducts full NI contributions from the employee's salary, but remits to the DSS only the appropriate reduced rate contribution. The balance is paid directly into the scheme's protected rights fund. There are stringent regulations requiring the administrator of such a scheme to ensure that the contributions are paid across to the scheme by the middle of each month, and to notify the DSS immediately if they are not so paid. In the case of the PP, however, the member's NI contributions paid to the DSS are at the full rate, and the DSS subsequently remits the rebate to the PP provider. This curious distinction between the two types of scheme becomes important when one realises that the occupational scheme can receive its funds to invest considerably earlier than a comparable PP arrangement: even allowing for the time difference caused by the convoluted path the money takes before reaching the PP, the process is often lengthened by the lethargy which can sometimes characterise the payment of the rebate by the DSS.

One further difference currently exists between these two types of arrangement. The Government, in an attempt to encourage the take-up of PPs, currently provides an incentive payment of 1 per cent of a member's earnings between the LEL and the upper earnings limit (UEL) to a PP, in respect of members who are aged 30 and above. The incentive is not payable to members of any other contracted-out arrangement.

Following the recommendations of the White Paper on 'Security, equality choice: the future for pensions' the 1995 Pensions Act has introduced the possibility of a new regime for contracting-out from 1997. Its proposals (which are considered in Chapter 12) are aimed at simplifying contracting-out requirements and procedures for benefits accruing post-1997. However, it leaves in place the current complexities for contracted out benefits accruing pre-1997.

2.9 Unapproved schemes

These are schemes which provide benefits which are inconsistent with Inland Revenue approval regimes and are therefore not able to qualify for the preferential tax concessions associated with formal approval. They are usually used to provide benefits on earnings above the earnings cap. The whole area of unapproved schemes is dealt with in Chapter 11.

B Identifying your needs

Before employees can be provided with a pension benefit, the company's aims and objectives in having a pension scheme must be identified. The type of scheme which most suits the company's and employees' current and future needs and costs must be decided on and how much authority and responsibility the company wishes (and indeed will be allowed) to delegate to others – notably the trustees – must be established. Progress in this is more effectively achieved by appointing advisers: some considerations for this are looked at in Chapter 3. Chapter 4 discusses how to design the scheme and Chapter 5 considers the balance of power.

3 Choosing your advisers

Knowing the types of scheme available does not help much in deciding the design most suited to your company. Your advisers can help, but they must first be chosen. Where do you start? Probably the best approach is to examine the many and varied duties of the professional advisers who could be involved in the running of your scheme and take account of both the trustees' role and the company's needs – not forgetting or overestimating the in-house services you can already provide.

For a medium-sized self-administered pension scheme the list of professional advisers could be as follows:

1. Pensions consultant.
2. Consulting actuary.
3. Legal adviser.
4. Investment consultant.
5. Auditor.
6. Investment manager.
7. Scheme administrator.

The size of the scheme and the interests and abilities of your own employees will determine your approach to the appointment of advisers.

In a smaller scheme all the advisers listed above, apart from the auditor, may come from an insurance company but it is always advantageous to obtain independent advice on the type of insurance contracts available, the security of the insurance companies and the quality of their administration. Furthermore the insured contract may satisfy many but not all of your needs, and as these needs and legislation change you may find the insurance approach becomes too restrictive and inflexible. Inevitably insurance companies provide a standardised service to numerous pension schemes and there is less scope to tailor their product to your needs. Equally, there is a danger that you too readily adapt your needs to what they can provide. Independent advice from a pensions consultant is therefore always advisable. Where you are normally satisfied with the services of the insurance company, advice from a pensions consultant can be used on an *ad hoc* basis. The larger firms of consultants offer the full range of services, normally with the exception of investment fund management and auditing, and are prepared to provide any one or all of the services as required.

The type of scheme you operate – final salary or money purchase, contracted-out or not, self-administered or insured, contributory or not – will again influence the advisory services required. Nevertheless, it is the consultant who plays a key role in the establishment and running of the scheme at all stages and his or her selection and appointment are crucial. The consultant may also be your actuary but we shall initially emphasise the differences between the two roles before considering the effectiveness of a combined role.

3.1 Pensions consultancy

The first important step in establishing your scheme is the appointment of the pensions consultant, who will then be able to work with you to design or review the benefit structures and to help you with the appointment of the other advisers.

Essentially, therefore, he or she will be your main external point of contact in connection with the running of your scheme. He or she will coordinate the external services provided to you, possibly even interpreting the more technical advice provided by the other advisers to the scheme. As such you will depend on the following attributes:

1. Integrity – do you feel you can trust and relate to your consultant?
2. Impartiality – to whom does the consultant report: trustees, company or both? Is this a problem? Does he or she favour final salary schemes? What pressures are put on the consultant within his or her organisation?
3. Knowledge, qualifications (by examination or otherwise) and experience – variety of clients, previous employers and years within the industry. Provided there is sufficient expertise within the organisation, you may prefer someone with more flair and dynamism, rather than technical ability, as your main contact.
4. Communication skills – the consultant will need to explain and present complex concepts to your board, the trustees and members.
5. Quality – you know it when you have got it. Look at his or her style, approach, reports, response to questions.
6. Support staff – how many are there? Who are they? Are they taking professional exams? How frequently will you and your staff meet them?
7. Understanding of and involvement in your organisation – is there a genuine interest? Can the consultant identify your business needs and relate them to your pension package? Does he or she see your report and accounts, staff magazine and sales literature?
8. Availability – how heavily involved is the consultant in the management of the organisation or in industry bodies such as National Association of Pension Funds, Society of Pensions Consultants or Association of Consulting Actuaries?

9. Organisational skills – your consultant will need to be able to organise the various advisers involved and possibly some of your own personnel as well as his or her own work. He or she will need to demonstrate preparedness for meetings, completed research and that he or she is in control.

It is therefore important that you meet your consultant and the rest of the team before making the appointment. This would seem to be an obvious statement but there are still some pensions consultancy organisations with sales teams who develop the contact, complete the sale and only then introduce the servicing team.

The individual consultant is inextricably linked to the organisation for whom he or she works, so let us first consider this organisation. Size to some may be a significant factor. Arguably the larger consultancies can offer greater security but even they can be taken over. In any merger or acquisition there is initial uncertainty and turmoil and the merging of two corporate cultures can lead to a new organisation with a different approach from that which you had originally required. Technical and research facilities are normally more abundant in the larger organisations and can therefore lead to the provision of more technical support in the form of periodicals and briefings. They have to be paid for and are normally reflected in the fees charged.

Information on the number of clients (and their relative size) will be of value. If your own scheme is significantly larger than any of the others being looked after by the consultancy, then you may be given pride of place with a fast service. However, being a large fish in a small sea has its downside, particularly when you require a considerable commitment over a short period of time, such as occurs during an acquisition or when a major benefits review is being implemented. This should not necessarily mean the demise of your regular consultant, but perhaps the appointment of a second consultancy organisation to help in that specific project.

On the other hand, for some small to medium-sized pension schemes there is the fear that being looked after by a large multinational consultancy may be expensive – you could be paying indirectly for services you may never need. Furthermore, there is the question of the level of priority that will be given to your scheme, particularly if the consultant has some larger clients. A high quality, professional consultant will always take the view that he or she will provide the best possible advice, in a timely manner, irrespective of the size of the scheme.

How many clients does the consultancy advise? Can the consultancy provide you with a breakdown of the different services provided to those clients? For example, if you want advice on the design, implementation and running of a flexible benefits programme you must ask your potential advisers about their experience and clients in this area. They could well have many clients where they provide consultancy advice but none where they are actually doing the administration. You need to know this and to be reassured that they are able to provide an effective administration service before they are appointed. It can be beneficial to be in at the development stages of a new product or service with your consultants. They may take far more notice of your specific requirements and you may benefit from reduced fees. Inevitably in developing new services there will be teething problems and you should not underestimate their impact on your organisation.

Consider the revenue and profitability of the consultancy. What is its mix of business? If it is not profitable, are you destined for increasing fee rates or a contracting service?

Location may also be a consideration. Local service can be an advantage but if the local office cannot provide the full range of services you require, you may be heavily dependent on back-up from another office. This can often work satisfactorily, but you need to investigate the two offices involved and the relationship between them.

Quality and timeliness of service are difficult to assess. One indication can be the proportion of professionally qualified staff and trainees. It is more important to talk to existing clients, since there should be some who are receiving the same range of services and operate the same size of scheme as you and some who are being looked after by the same consultant as you would be. The objective must be to identify the strengths and weaknesses of the consultancy team you will be appointing with the aim of appointing an organisation whose strengths complement your own and whose weaknesses you are not only aware of but can accommodate or control.

It is useful to be able to discuss the organisational structure of the consultancy firm. How senior is your consultant? To whom does he or she report? How frequently will you have the opportunity of discussing service issues with more senior personnel? Such people have the advantage of not being involved in the detail and may therefore be able to take a more strategic view of how your benefits packages can adapt to the changing nature of the environment in which you work and your longer-term business plans. Reviewing the services provided and the future benefit needs is considered in more detail in Chapter 10.

The influences that are brought to bear on consultancy organisations are many and varied. Several of the larger consultancies are owned by companies such as insurance brokers and banks, others continue to emphasise their independence and partnership status or are wholly owned by their senior staff. Commercially those who are linked to other organisations have a far wider range of potential business contacts. They are, however, often sensitive to their parent companies' influence and potential interference in the way the consultancy conducts its business. This can sometimes impact upon the service provided by the consultancy, and shareholders' short term interests may from time to time be more in evidence. However, these ownership issues have more impact on the style than the quality of the consultancy service.

Obviously your company and trustees will require investment advice from time to time and may wish to provide retirement or redundancy counselling. You may prefer to use a different organisation from your normal pensions consultants on the grounds of not putting all your eggs in one basket; the advice to company, to trustees and to individuals could then be separate. However, if the company or trustees encourage this service they should go through the same process in assessing the organisation and individuals providing the advice. All such investment advice must be conducted within the requirements of the Financial Services Act. At present authorisation of organisations providing investment advice must be through one of the following:

1. SIB – Securities and Investment Board.
2. IMRO – Investment Managers Regulatory Organisation.
3. RPB – recognised professional bodies, e.g. Law Society, Institute of Actuaries, Institute of Chartered Accountants.
4. PIA – Personal Investment Authority.

Although some aspects of the Financial Services Act and the operation of the above bodies may be considered over-bureaucratic, much is good business sense and goes a long way to ensure that corporate and individual clients are properly advised and that all aspects of their investment requirements are carefully considered and taken into account.

The compliance rules for each of the above organisations are perhaps slightly different, but with the same theme. You may find it instructive to ask your potential consultancy with which organisation it is registered. How frequently does its compliance officer visit the offices and examine files? When was the last formal visit from its regulatory body? What were the findings? Has it been fined or asked to reinstate client monies as a consequence of incorrect advice?

No organisation is perfect and all will from time to time have been subject to criticisms from their regulatory body. A positive reaction to such criticisms – identifying if there are any underlying problems and dealing with those in a positive and constructive manner – is more reassuring.

Errors inevitably do occur from time to time. Despite your expectations and possibly their claims, your consultancy is not superhuman. So how does it handle clients' claims against it? Asking about professional indemnity insurance may solicit some useful information. How many insurance claims did it have last year? How many were or are in the process of being settled? What insurance is in place, both in terms of the amount self-insured and the maximum cover?

There are three ways of losing money – horses, women and taking the advice of experts:

>   horses – that is the quickest;
>   women – that is the most pleasant;
>   but taking the advice of an expert – that is the most certain.

Georges Pompidou

Fees are obviously a very important consideration but it is surprising how often no clear specification for the ongoing work is given. There is a variety of ways of expressing fees. It is often suggested that operating on a time–cost basis leaves you to decide as and when you need to involve your consultant. On the other hand, it can stifle initiative and limit the contact you have with your consultant.

Fixed fees and retainers have the advantage of certainty but need considerable clarification regarding the work being undertaken. There is often the fear that when a fixed fee is paid, the work actually done is on a time spent basis, or alternatively that the service during the year deteriorates as the fixed fee is used up.

Commissions may be taken instead of, on top of or offsetting fees. What are these commissions? How frequently are they are paid? Are they always openly declared? There are horror stories within the industry about organisations taking very large commissions for setting up the pension scheme and giving little or no service subsequently because the renewal commission is very small and therefore would not support a continuing service. Try to see a detailed specification of the work to be done, the fees (and any offsetting commissions) to be charged and supporting documentation issued with the fee invoice giving a breakdown of the work done. Even where your consultancy is operating on commission or a fixed fee, it is useful to have information regarding the work done and time spent. All too often clients underestimate the work done and the complexities involved.

Comparing fee quotations is fraught with difficulties, but you should take into account items such as the following:

1. Commissions.
2. Time spent in addition to the fixed fee.
3. Charges for computer and secretarial time.
4. Charges for travel time and disbursements.
5. Charges for printing.
6. Charges for additional presentations.

The comparison is rarely a perfect science but greater clarification can be obtained if you provide a brief specification for all to quote against. Give details of the scheme, its benefits, the services you require, the expected number of meetings, all anticipated commissions to be estimated and offset. It often helps.

Eliminating the highest and lowest fee quotation can be unwise. Give each an opportunity to comment – preferably at a meeting – on the quotation and how it compares. The lowest quotation may have taken account of commissions and be assuming that your organisation will be more heavily involved in the day-to-day administration and will require very few meetings, all in its offices. The highest quotation may reflect the opposite approach.

If you still have difficulty assessing the quotation/proposal you may ask a different organisation, or one that has already quoted, to provide an objective assessment of the other quotations – a good test of its impartial objectivity!

The consultancy that you eventually appoint will hopefully be with you for many years, reflecting the long-term relationship that is desirable in running your scheme. It is essentially a partnership, but nevertheless benefits from a period of courtship and honeymoon. Whilst fees may be one of the determining factors in your decision they should not be the sole determinant. When compared with the scheme's assets under management or the regular contributions being paid they represent a very small proportion of the costs of running the scheme.

Obviously your preferred consultants must be able to demonstrate value for money and added value in the service they are undertaking. Quality and the ability of your consultant and his or her organisation to identify your current and future needs and to work with you in partnership to achieve these aims are far more important.

3.2 The actuary

The actuary will certainly be one of the most important of all your professional advisers, advising on the cost of your pension scheme (particularly for a final salary arrangement) to the company, the trustees and members, the range of benefits and options such as early retirement, and the liability profile of your scheme for investment and cash-flow purposes. In some organisations the actuary will be your pensions consultant as well. In others, the roles are split. If the two roles are undertaken by the actuary, you need to consider whether he or she will have sufficient time to deal with all your requirements and the expertise to handle such items as communication and presentations to members, simplifying complex issues and coordinating the various services provided and professional advisers involved. Many actuaries do have the necessary skills – some unfortunately do not.

Separating the roles can be beneficial, particularly where the actuary and consultant work closely together and complement each other. If they do not you may obtain conflicting advice, delays because of communication problems, and higher fees, for example where the consultant continually has to update the actuary. Furthermore, if you, and particularly your finance director, are not building a strong relationship with your actuary, he or she may not get to understand your short- and long-term financing objectives for the scheme. Providing consultancy from one office and actuarial from another can cause confusion and delays if the roles and communication channels are not well established.

Where the team approach is genuinely operated within the appointed consultancy organisation and communication skills are good, either approach works, and the decision may be based on personal preference and costs. Should one of the senior team members leave, you do at least have the considerable advantage of continuity from the other members.

The Institute and Faculty of Actuaries operate a series of Guidance Notes covering actuarial practice and in particular Guidance Note 9 deals with the contents of actuarial reports on the valuation of a pension scheme. These professional standards control the minimum content of the report, not the style, and you may find a brief examination of the actuarial report to be either instructive or confusing.

There is certainly a lot of routine calculation in much actuarial work and the extent to which this is standardised and computerised is worth considering as it can substantially reduce your costs. An example is the calculation of individual transfer values. Probably 80 per cent of these for most schemes are complex calculations but they are capable of being structured for ease of manual or computer calculation. If more expensive actuarial staff are doing these calculations, you should ask for the reason as you may pay the cost.

The actuary's involvement in the investment process should also be considered. He or she will work closely with the investment manager to establish the investment needs following the investigation of the scheme's liability profile and the future cash flows. Where, for example, the scheme is taking a contribution holiday and there are several senior employees due to retire, there may not be sufficient cash to provide the cash sums at retirement. Anticipating this in advance can avoid the necessity of selling stock which would otherwise have been held and so suffering the cost of sales, possibly at a time when the market is at a low. The maturity of your scheme, the extent to which any surplus or deficit exists and the consequent funding policy, together with the investment process, are items which your actuary, pensions consultant or investment consultant should take into account in the advice they give. Questioning the actuary on such areas can lead to some fascinating responses!

3.3 Investment consultant

The company (as well as the trustees) will certainly want to know the success of the investment managers in terms of the sustainable investment returns they are achieving and the risks they are taking. Most of the leading firms of consulting actuaries and consultants provide such a measurement service either directly or through a separate organisation. Your actuary will normally be involved in this process and so too may a specialist investment consultant. Once again, before appointment, review the standard reports that are provided. Question the investment consultant and actuary on market trends and comparison with industry indices and peer groups.

The investment consultant is at the forefront at times of reappraisal of investment strategy and appointment of new investment managers. His or her knowledge and understanding of the markets and the fund managers' organisations must be up to date and readily communicable. The investment consultant must, when working with the actuary, be able to interpret the results of any asset/liability and asset allocation modelling that may be undertaken.

3.4 The legal adviser

Much of the legal and documentation work associated with the establishment and running of your pension scheme can be done by your appointed firm of pensions consultants or consulting actuaries. Certainly drafting documents and amending deeds is for many a routine matter. However, it is once again useful to determine how much of the documentation specialist's work is with his or her own company's standard documents and how much is with non-standards, which can be more time-consuming and complex. If most of the work is with own standard documents, you may be encouraged to re-write your own documents to reflect these standards. The need for regular updates has been noted in the report from the Pensions Law Review Committee (the Goode Committee Report) and endorsed by the Government's White Paper and 1995 Pensions Act and is certainly to be welcomed. The fees for the initial work in redrafting or drafting a trust deed and preparing documentation for submission to the Pension Schemes Office (PSO) and the Occupational Pensions Board (OPB) can be large, but it is normally a very infrequent occurrence and the trustees, members and advisers all benefit substantially from having an up-to-date set of rules. Provided the documentation is done well, subsequent legal changes can be kept to a minimum and costs thereby contained.

However, you should still check the need for such a re-write. The legal requirements under the various social security and finance acts together with amendments, and the discretionary practice of the PSO, ensure a continuing complexity which needs the technical skills of a documentation expert and can warrant the appointment of a lawyer with practical pensions experience. Pensions are becoming more closely linked with employment issues – particularly in European law – and your pensions lawyer will need to be expert in these areas as well.

Your legal adviser will probably be used more on a consulting basis and for engrossing deeds or advising when disputes occur. Fees will almost invariably reflect the time spent and complexity of the work undertaken.

3.5 Auditors

The Occupational Pension Schemes (Disclosure of Information) Regulations 1986 (SI 1986/1046) and subsequent amendments require certain information to be provided to members of pension schemes and set timescales for the provision of such information. In particular, the trustees' report and accounts must be available within twelve months of the end of the scheme year.

However, conflicts do arise. Your company may consider best practice to be to use the company's auditors for the pension scheme audit. Not only does this introduce the concern regarding the appointment of independent advisers to the scheme (and this will be considered later) but it raises the question of priority given to the work. Your company pays a large fee to its auditors; the pension scheme audit fees are normally small in comparison. Consequently, all too often the scheme audit is given a low priority. Furthermore, many of the smaller auditing firms have limited experience of pension scheme accounts and audits and they often send junior articled clerks to do the initial work. The first job therefore is to educate the articled clerk in pensions terminology and the working of pension schemes. This can be a slow and expensive task for you and your administrators.

In appointing pension scheme auditors, therefore, you should ensure that timetables are set and agreed. If because of company audit they are unable to meet the necessary deadlines, you may have to consider the alternative of a separate audit practice to do the pensions scheme audit. It is certainly worth while asking prospective scheme auditors about the audit procedures they operate for pension scheme accounts and the number of pension scheme clients they look after.

The audit process is more important than ever following the Maxwell scandal of 1992. This is discussed again in Chapter 12 where the requirements of the Government's White Paper and 1995 Pensions Act are considered. However, in appointing your auditors, you should always ask them to outline the audit process and checks they make on calculations, contributions, investment proceeds and security.

3.6 Investment managers

Your consultant or actuary and investment consultant will certainly be greatly involved in the appointment of your investment manager or managers, including surveyors if you are large enough to invest directly in property. The size of funds under management will determine whether you appoint internal or external fund managers. The types of investment services available are covered in Chapter 7. For self-administered schemes normal practice would be to invest in unitised managed or specialist funds where the scheme is less than £10 million and give consideration to direct investments via the Stock Exchange where funds are more than £10 million and expanding. (The £10m limit is merely a guide and depends on the type, maturity, cash-flow and funding level of the scheme, as well as risk factors and performance requirements.)

The process of selection of your fund managers should start with an assessment of the risk–return requirements, including asset/liability considerations and company and trustees' perspectives, bearing in mind any restrictions that may be contained in the scheme rules. Your consultant will then identify which of the numerous fund managers are best able to satisfy those needs. He or she will help prepare a brief to issue to a small number of those fund managers, so enabling them to prepare their presentation to the trustees and company. Unless you are very clear on your requirements for a fund manager it is advisable to look at a range of organisations, such as merchant banks, stockbrokers, specialist fund managers and insurance companies.

Your prospective fund manager will make a presentation to you. This should include the following:

1. Performance and risk.
2. Long- and short-term strategy.
3. Reporting procedures, including fund valuations and market summaries.
4. Accounting and tax reclamation.
5. Custody of stock holdings.
6. Charges including offsetting brokerage fees.

The presentation should allow plenty of time for questions and discussions. Sometimes companies and trustees try to cover too many presentations in one day. Two or three are normally sufficient if you want time to consider the discussions in detail. More information on investment strategies is included in Chapter 7 and a brief checklist of questions to ask your fund manager is included at the end of this chapter (Checklist 2).

Choosing your investment manager is an elimination process. It must be done thoroughly and methodically if you are to appoint a successful manager who can satisfy the trustees' and company's needs. Make sure that you will have the opportunity of regularly meeting your fund manager and not one of the investment house's salespeople.

Before confirmation of appointment you should take the opportunity of looking at the standard investment manager agreement that you will be asked to sign: it may be full of jargon and very confusing. With your consultant you can review the services offered to ensure that nothing has been overlooked. You may also wish to include as part of the agreement, or in a separate letter, performance targets and objectives (these are considered in Chapter 7).

Performance-related fees are sometimes worthy of consideration rather than a percentage of funds under management. However, there can be hidden fees particularly where the manager is investing in numerous in-house unitised funds and taking commissions on turnover of stock, and your consultant should help you through this.

3.7 Advisers: to whom?

The pension scheme is a partnership between the members and the company. Both are beneficiaries: the former more directly, but the latter is unlikely to set up a pension scheme if there is no benefit to be gained from it, for example, goodwill, increased productivity and retention of staff, and it would normally be the remainderman taking any remaining surplus when the scheme has been wound-up.

The day-to-day operation of your pension scheme will require advice from your chosen professionals. For all but the very large schemes one set of advisers is appointed to cover the needs of both the company and trustees, and problems of conflict rarely occur. Where, however, they do arise, it is important that you have identified to whom your regular consultants normally report. The Government's White Paper and 1995 Pensions Act followed the Goode Committee recommendations requiring that trustees should have the responsibility for appointing advisers to the scheme. There may therefore be more occasions when the company will have to appoint separate advisers in the event of a conflict. However, currently in many Trust Deed and Rules the appointment of some or all of the advisers rests with the company or jointly with the trustees.

Not only is it important to check, it is also essential from the outset that the advisers know to whom they are principally reporting. There should be clear written terms of reference for advisers. Certainly if you have chosen wisely, your professional advisers will ensure that the advice they give is tailored to reflect the trustees' role or the company's interests and where there is a potential conflict they will ensure this is brought to the attention of all parties involved. In the vast majority of cases such conflicts are sensibly discussed and resolved.

3.8 Scheme administrator

The smooth day-to-day running of the pension scheme is considered by many to be more important than any other aspects. Delays in setting up pension benefits or making payments to leavers or spouses after a member's death give the scheme and company a bad name. Incorrect benefit statements, poor communications and out-of-date booklets cause confusion and can lead to mistrust if such errors and delays continue.

Choosing an administrator is no different in practice from choosing your pensions consultant or actuary. You have three options:

1. To recruit a team of pensions administrators into your own organisation. This is really a practical option only for the very large pension schemes and you would need to work very closely with your consultant to consider the organisational structure. The major advantage is one of total control in terms of service and cost. Probably the biggest concern occurs when you are unable to provide career development and a small number but a large proportion of your administration team moves on. During the recruitment period your service to members deteriorates.
2. To appoint external administrators completely separate from your other advisers. Provided their service is very good this can work extremely well, although you should be conscious of the potential communication problems between the consultant, actuary and administrator if all are employed by different organisations. This may put an additional coordinating responsibility on your shoulders or increase one or more parties' costs – and your expenses.
3. To appoint external administrators who are part of your consultant's or actuary's organisation.

The procedures you go through and the items you are looking for are similar irrespective of the type of external administrator you appoint, and many aspects apply equally to your in-house pensions administrator. Many of them have already been considered above in relation to the appointment of your pensions consultant and his or her organisation, so here we shall concentrate on the specific administration considerations.

There is some very sophisticated computer software available for pensions administration and it is all too easy to be impressed by it. The saying 'rubbish in, rubbish out' is just as true for computerised pensions administration as anywhere else. You are looking for a total administration service: computer software is merely a tool which helps in the provision of the service.

Are there areas of the administration that you would prefer to do within your own organisation, such as running the scheme's bank account, paying pensions and other benefits? Do not try to do too much initially. It is false economy and can easily introduce further delays. Your aim should be to agree procedures and timescales and monitor performance (this will be covered in Chapters 6 and 10).

You should be given a draft administration manual which will identify what your payroll and personnel departments will be required to do as part of the pensions administration process. It should also itemise what the external pensions manager will do, the agreed timescales, contacts and standard letters. Do you want standard letters to be in your company style?

Have you considered benefits statements in your corporate style? Many administrators will provide considerable flexibility in this area.

Administration fees are usually of the order of half the total cost of all fees associated with the running of your pension scheme. The most common fee arrangement would be a fixed fee with additional charges for unexpected work such as a major redundancy programme or the merging of schemes following an acquisition. Fee quotations for administration services can be very complex and confusing. Some items will be included in a fixed fee, others vary depending on usage, still more on initial 'set up' or 'take on' charges for one year or spread over three years. Where you are considering an administration service which is independent of your other advisers you should request a management agreement detailing procedures, timescales and costs.

Checklist 3 at the end of this chapter covers all the basic aspects of administration. This should help to ensure you do not fail to consider the main items required from the administration service. However, by far the greatest help in this very difficult decision will be your discussions with existing clients. Considering cost at the expense of quality is dangerous. You should choose a very good administrator and then attempt to negotiate a sensible cost. The opposite approach rarely works.

The bitterness of low quality lasts long after the sweetness of low price.

3.9 Trustees

The duties and role of trustees are the subject of numerous textbooks and are not considered here. The 1995 Pensions Act has adopted most of the Government's White Paper recommendations concerning the number and appointment of member-nominated trustees. Trustees are to be given more powers in the appointment of advisers and the running of schemes. The removal of member-nominated trustees will only be possible by a unanimous decision of all the other trustees and the Regulator set up under the Act should be notified. Clearly, therefore, the selection process and training of trustees must be given very careful consideration.

Goode and the White Paper rejected compulsory independent trustees for ongoing schemes as there are insufficient candidates for the role. Many organisations can provide independent trusteeship. This can be useful to demonstrate impartiality, particularly when exercising trustees' discretion. But beware: appointing an independent trustee can transfer too many powers outside the control of the company, leading to inflexibility when changes may be required.

Some consultancy practices provide trustee services when appointed as consultant. Such a service can never be independent or impartial, and smacks of poacher turned gamekeeper. The argument for this approach is that it binds the consultancy to the trustees: they are all liable for the decisions made. However, objectivity can be difficult to maintain, particularly where the consultancy is also providing actuarial, documentation and administration services. Indeed the 1995 Pensions Act has made it clear that neither the actuary nor the auditor can act as trustees. Further clarification is, however, awaited regarding the roles which employers of actuaries and auditors can play. If a truly independent trustee is required, then one must be appointed from either a separate consultancy, trustee company or other professional body (normally solicitors) who are in no other way associated with your organisation.

Initially at least the company will appoint some of the trustees and be involved in the procedures for appointing member-nominated trustees. It is always important to ensure that the trustees are aware of their general duties and responsibilities and their more specific powers as enshrined in the Trust Deed and Rules. Regular trustee training is therefore to be encouraged. Furthermore, the pensions consultant should always attend trustees' meetings to ensure they are fully aware of their duties, discretions, the rule of law and good practice.

It is important from the company's point of view that you take as much trouble over the appointment of your scheme trustees as you do with the appointment of advisers and senior personnel.

Checklist 1   Professional advisers

Organisation
- partnership or limited company
- major shareholders
- major business activities
- independence
- management structure

Quality and style
- proportion of qualified   actuaries
                             pensions consultants
                             accountants
                             lawyers
- policy towards staff training and continuous professional development
- list of existing clients to contact
- team or individual approach
- literature and draft reports

Size
- revenues and profits
- number of clients
- clients gained and lost
- number of offices
- number of employees, preferably by office

Services provided
- administration   – record keeping
                         – secretarial/accounts
                         – payment of pensions
- actuarial
- documentation
- communications
- general consultancy

Fees
- time spent or fixed fee
- chargeable rates
- commissions   – on what contracts?
                        – how much are they?
- draft agreement identifying services
- travel time and computer time
- frequency of invoicing
- breakdown of fees

Personnel
- would you employ?
- experience and professional qualifications
- knowledge and expertise
- communication skills
- support staff – number and quality
- meet the team and the management

Checklist 2   Investment manager

These items are in addition to those on the Professional Advisers checklist.

Organisation
- nature of bank, merchant bank, life office, investment trust, etc.
- number of managers employed, background, age and experience
- how long has it been managing pension fund investments?

Size
- total assets under management
- range of funds and investment services available
- distribution of size of client funds under management

Investment philosophy
- attitude to different sectors (equities, gilts, property, overseas, etc.)
- approach to sector analysis and stock selection
- research – internal resources or bought in from stockbrokers?
- decision-making process – too heavily dependent on one or two senior personnel or considerable freedom for investment managers?
- how is overall investment strategy determined?

Administration
- registration – in whose name is stock held?
- is there a separate custodian?
- collection of interest, dividends and tax
- rights and scrip issues
- how frequent are reports and valuations – are they clear and summarised?
- how frequently will the manager visit the trustees to report progress?
- banking services
- who will report to trustees?

Investment performance
- performance record and consistency
- comparisons with peer group and industry indices
- variability of performance between fund managers within the organisation and between agreed performance targets, benchmarks and period over which performance is to be measured

Fees
- fixed fee, fee based on assets under management, performance-related fee
- commission on Stock Exchange dealings
- charges for internal specialist funds

Checklist 3   Pensions administrator

These items are in addition to those in the Professional Advisers checklist.

Administration procedures
- draft administration manual
- basic record-keeping and calculations
- dealing with members' queries
- running scheme bank account
- dealing with PSO, OPB and DSS queries
- arranging death-in-service and other insurances
- calculating benefits and advising members
- scheme accounts to audit stage

Turnaround times
- benefit statements
- leavers
- transfer values
- deaths
- early retirements
- new entrants

Initial transfer of data
- cost and timescale

Initial setting up of system
- cost and timescale

Management/agreement fee

4 Designing the scheme

When setting up a new scheme, once the advisers have been appointed, the next step is to work with them to design the benefit structure appropriate to the company and its employees. Without going through this careful planning stage, you are likely to end up with a scheme which costs the company too much money and yet still does not provide appropriate benefits for your workforce. Unfortunately, many of the pension schemes which are in existence today were set up by employers with no clear idea of what they were intended to achieve. If yours is just such a scheme, this process is equally valid as a review. With changing business, legal and social environments your existing scheme's benefit structure may from time to time not satisfy the needs of members or the business, and redesigning the scheme becomes necessary.

A systematic approach starting with an analysis of the employee profile and taking account of both the employer's and employees' needs is likely to lead to the most appropriate scheme. There is no 'best' design for a pension scheme. In any situation the scheme which most closely meets the aspirations of employees and employer is the best. An attitudinal survey of employees can be of value particularly if you are reviewing the whole benefit package.

4.1 Initial considerations

4.1.1 Work profile

Working practices continue to adapt to changing business needs. The introduction of short-term contracts, franchising and 'homeworking' and the ever-increasing use of technology are changing employment attitudes; for many there is no longer the cradle-to-grave mentality. Nowadays many organisations design the remuneration package to suit the current needs of employees and to provide more immediate direct rewards for their efforts.

As an organisation you may operate a unistatus or a tiered approach to benefits. Either way the benefits provided need to reflect the changing needs of the employees and the business and the environment in which you operate. A survey of pension provision within the industry or location in which you operate can be instructive.

4.1.2 Employee profile

You need to look at the employee profile of your company. The needs of a large mature employer with a long-serving workforce, possibly the dominant employer in the community in which it is based, are different from those of a young company with high employee turnover from small groups spread throughout the country. To show the pattern of employment, an age, sex, marital and service analysis of the current workforce should be performed. When combined with the turnover statistics, the pattern of employment is shown and you can then consider whether the pattern is changing or is likely to change significantly in the future.

4.1.3 Pension scheme objective

Taking account of the employment pattern, you should then consider what the objective of the pension scheme will be. Examples are as follows:

1. To provide a specific level of retirement income.
2. To encourage employees to save for retirement.
3. To enable the employer to hire the required types of employees.
4. To reward long service.
5. To tax shelter a portion of remuneration.
6. To provide protection in the event of death or ill health.

These are merely some of the objectives put forward by companies and individuals, and demonstrate the widely differing viewpoints of those involved in pension schemes. They are all legitimate objectives and you will probably find that you will be seeking to meet more than one of these when designing your own scheme.

4.1.4 Target retirement income

An essential part of the design process of a pension scheme must be an assessment of the target retirement income it is expected to provide for members. In considering this, the overall expected income of pensioners must be kept in mind. This means taking account of the expected state pensions to be received, both from the state basic scheme and from SERPS. You should consider the ability of a member who has worked for the company for a reasonable number of years to enjoy an appropriate standard of living in retirement which is not out of proportion to his or her standard of living while in employment, i.e. neither too high nor too low. This means that in considering income before and after retirement the effects of taxation and expenses also need to be taken into account.

The main areas of reduction in expenditure after retirement are NI contributions (up to 10 per cent of earnings), pension scheme contributions and travel expenses. Other items which are not common to all but can be significant are mortgage payments, children's education and working clothes. The level of taxation is also slightly lower due to increased personal allowances for those over state pension age. The effect of these items varies widely but taken as a whole they clearly reduce the level of gross income required in retirement for individuals to maintain their standards of living.

On the other hand, however, the individual may incur higher costs in other areas, such as increased heating, lighting and food through being at home for most of the day. In addition, one significant item of cost which is often overlooked is the running of a car, where the employee was provided with a car by the company while in employment. The running and depreciation costs connected with a motor car are significant and can constitute an unexpectedly large drain on retirement income. Another area which should be considered is the need for long-term care after retirement – this is an ever-increasing cost.

4.2 The defined benefit scheme

We now move on to the design of specific aspects of the scheme structure. The benefit design should of course not be considered in isolation from the costs of providing those benefits. Your adviser, and in particular the actuary, will be able to provide cost estimates for each of the variations of the elements involved in the design process.

4.2.1 Eligibility

Entry into the pension scheme may be immediate, coinciding with entry into service with the company, or it may be delayed for a period, possibly being subject to the employee achieving a given age and/or status. The options are numerous and your final choice may be based on one or more factors such as the following:

1. The likelihood that employees, if not immediately allowed into the scheme, will effect their own personal pension arrangements in preference, and subsequently they will not want to switch over once they become eligible for membership of the pension scheme.
2. If members are required to contribute, the extent to which younger employees will have other more pressing uses for their income, such as house purchase, etc.
3. Staff turnover rates. If turnover is high in the first few years of employment, you may wish to defer employees' eligibility to join until the end of that period. For those who leave prior to completion of this waiting period, the company will not have incurred the unnecessary administration connected with the employee entering and then leaving

the scheme within a relatively short period. Once the member has entered at the end of the waiting period, the scheme may then count the time spent in the waiting period as though the employee had been a member of the scheme during that time (although if the waiting period is recognised in this way, then the member's benefit on subsequent leaving will be calculated as though the member had entered the scheme at the beginning of the waiting period).

4. Since April 1988 it has not been possible to make membership of the scheme compulsory. However many companies use the principle of inertia to ensure a high proportion of new entrants. The company pension scheme is usually good and potential members are advised of the benefits and that it will be assumed they will join unless the company hears to the contrary – in writing. Recent evidence showed that the take-up rate for schemes with such a feature is higher than for those where entry involves a deliberate decision to join.

5. It may be more appropriate to grant immediate entry to older and/or more senior employees who have been recruited from another company in mid-career. They will probably have enjoyed membership of a pension scheme in respect of their previous employment and may not be prepared to serve a waiting period before becoming eligible to join their new employer's scheme.

Where a waiting period is imposed, employers often nevertheless provide some form of life assurance cover during it. Since it is now no longer possible to make membership of a pension scheme compulsory as part of the employee's terms of employment, where life cover is provided during a waiting period, it can be designed to lapse at the end of that period if the employee chooses at that time not to join the scheme for full pension benefits.

You will also need to consider whether the pension scheme should be open to all employees. This is not just a case of having different benefit structures for works, staff and executive employees, but more fundamentally involves consideration of the position of part-time employees. In the past many schemes have specifically excluded part-time employees, but their inclusion is now becoming progressively more common and is a legal requirement following recent rulings of the European Court of Justice. The growth over recent years in the numbers of employees working on a part-time basis, and also the increasing interest being shown by the regulatory organs of the European Union have encouraged this. In particular, in the German 'Bilka Kaufhaus' case brought in 1986, the European Court of Justice ruled that a company was in breach of the rules against sex discrimination (see Chapter 12) where it did not allow its part-time employees to join its pension scheme, where a majority of those part-time employees were of one sex (in that case, women).

4.2.2 Normal pension date

The choice of a normal pension date will probably depend largely upon the normal practice in the industry involved and state pension age. Clearly the age selected will have a significant impact upon the cost of the scheme, and thus upon the profitability of the company. This cost aspect, translated into the effect on the benefit payable, is also of crucial importance from the employee's point of view. Since, as we mentioned above, it is usual to integrate the pension scheme benefit with the state pension entitlements to set an overall target retirement income for employees, it follows that the dates from which the state benefits are payable also have a significant effect on the equation. This is particularly so in respect of lower-paid employees where state benefits form a significant part of their total retirement income. The effect of the state benefits upon the whole is less pronounced for higher-paid employees because SERPS does not accrue in respect of any earnings above the UEL. Hence, all earnings above that level are left unpensioned by the state.

It is often appropriate and quite usual to provide a lower normal pension date in respect of executives and others whose employment places considerable physical or mental stress upon them. The Inland Revenue will generally allow a normal retirement age within the range 60–75. Any proposal to select a normal retirement age outside this range will usually require the specific approval of the Inland Revenue.

The most significant influence on the selection of normal retirement ages in recent years has been the intervention of European law. In this area it effectively now requires that male and female scheme members in comparable employments with the same employer must be entitled to equal treatment in respect of their membership of, and benefits from, the employer's pension scheme. One of the most fundamental aspects of this requirement is the need to equalise normal retirement ages. The problems associated with equalisation are dealt with in more detail in Chapter 12. However, we need to note here that considerable thought needs to be given to the selection of an appropriate normal retirement age, particularly in respect of lower-paid employees who may not be in a position financially to retire prior to the date from which they qualify for payment of their state pensions. Currently the state pension age remains at 65 for men and 60 for women. However, as is mentioned in Chapter 12, the Government has announced that the long-term intention is to fix it at age 65 for both sexes, with a gradual transition early next century. This means that scheme designers will have to give careful thought to this issue for some time to come. All these issues, together with the significantly higher cost of providing pensions for both sexes at age 60 as opposed to age 65, and taking account of the demographic trend of an older population with fewer young people entering the workforce, are combining to force the majority of employers to equalise normal retirement ages for both sexes at age 65.

4.2.3 Accrual rate

This is the fraction of the eventual pension which is earned by each year of service covered by the scheme. The choice of the accrual rate will depend upon the target pension which it is decided is appropriate for an average member of the scheme. At the top of the range, the accrual rate will be affected by the maximum pension permitted by the Inland Revenue under an approved pension scheme. For members who joined a scheme prior to 17 March 1987, the maximum is a pension of two-thirds, the final remuneration after ten years' pensionable service. After that date a member is only allowed the maximum for periods of service of at least twenty years. Fuller details of Inland Revenue limits are contained in Appendix 2. Below that maximum the scheme designer has total freedom to select an accrual rate which is considered appropriate. It is possible to introduce several tiers for different categories of membership. For example, a three-tier scheme might provide one-eightieth of final remuneration for each year of pensionable service for works employees, one-sixtieth for staff employees and one-forty-fifth for executives.

4.2.4 Pensionable salary and final pensionable salary

These are further important elements in the calculation of the pensions being earned. Pensionable salary could have many definitions. For example, it may include total earnings over the previous tax year, the fixed rate of basic salary at a particular date, basic salary plus the average of fluctuating emoluments over the last three years (where emoluments may include such items as commission, bonus and overtime earnings) or gross earnings in any pay period. It may even include taxable benefits in kind such as company cars. The selection of an appropriate definition will usually depend upon the significance of the earnings profile of the members concerned. For example, if overtime or bonuses do not form a substantial part of an employee's income, then they will probably be excluded. Conversely, commission and bonuses may form a substantial part of an employee's remuneration. That would point to the desirability of including such earnings in the definition of pensionable salary, although the company may wish to control its exposure to high pension costs arising from this source by placing a limit (either monetary or percentage) upon the commission or bonuses which can count towards pensionable salary.

Where the target retirement income includes state benefits, one common method of achieving integration is by deducting from the pensionable salary figure an amount which will reduce the final pension payable from the scheme by an amount equivalent to the expected state basic pension. It should be remembered, however, that state benefits are likely to be reduced over time and any integrated benefit formula needs to be carefully considered as a result.

Finally, the pensionable salary definition will have to take account of the earnings cap in appropriate cases. This issue is discussed more fully in Chapter 11.

The benefit payable from the scheme will usually be expressed in terms of final pensionable salary. Final pensionable salary will usually be arrived at by taking an average of an appropriate number of pensionable salaries leading up to the date of retirement. The purpose of averaging is to smooth out any fluctuations in pensionable salary figures prior to retirement. Such fluctuations often either take the form of a reduction as a member approaches retirement as a result of a tailing-off of his or her effectiveness and therefore particularly his or her bonus or commission earnings capacity, or alternatively (often in the case of senior executives) their particular expertise justifies an ever-growing remuneration which only stops at retirement.

There are several alternative definitions of final pensionable salary which are commonly used. Often schemes use basic remuneration in the year prior to retirement plus the average of fluctuating emoluments over the three years prior to retirement. Another common formula is the best average of three consecutive pensionable salaries ending in the ten years prior to retirement.

Specifically because of its effect of smoothing out fluctuations, the Inland Revenue requires that the final pensionable salary for directors who have a controlling interest in the sponsoring employer or who earn more than £100,000 a year is averaged over at least three years, to avoid these individuals manipulating their income to take unfair advantage of the rules and thereby enabling them to receive large pensions justified only by earnings inflated artificially just prior to retirement. The subsequent introduction of the earnings cap (see Chapter 11) has further complicated matters.

4.2.5 Pension increases

A pension may be paid for, possibly, two decades. Given the devastating effect which inflation can have on a fixed level of income, it is hardly surprising that considerable attention has been devoted to the question of increases to pensions in course of payment. It is therefore common to find pension increase provisions in schemes. These may be at the discretion of the trustees (perhaps with company approval) or guaranteed at a particular rate, or a combination of both.

Discretionary increases usually arise through the trustees using surplus assets disclosed in actuarial valuations – in effect a 'bonus' for members arising usually from the success of the investment manager. Guaranteed increases may be set at the rate of the increase in the Retail Prices Index (RPI), or at some lesser rate. The cost of full inflationary increases is very significant when inflation is at a high level. Consequently, the most common guaranteed level of pension increases is either 3 per cent per annum compound or limited price indexation, which are often viewed as a reasonable compromise giving some protection to pensions without unduly increasing the employer's costs.

Contracted-out schemes have to provide 3 per cent a year compound (or RPI increases, if less) pension increases on that part of the GMP which arises from service after 5 April 1988. In addition, there may be a further statutory requirement for all schemes (not just contracted-out) to provide increases in line with RPI up to 5 per cent (known colloquially as 'LPI') after an appointed day, which is suggested in the 1995 Pensions Act as being April 1997. These provisions are explained in more detail in Chapter 12.

4.2.6 Lump sum benefits

The Inland Revenue allows a member to obtain a lump sum from a pension scheme at retirement, subject to certain limits. This can either be provided through the exchange of some of the member's pension, or alternatively it can be on top of the pension. Either way, the cash sum will have a value in terms of an equivalent pension, which is then aggregated with the pension payable in addition, for the purpose of testing the total pension against Inland Revenue limits. The lump sum is payable free from tax under present legislation.

There is a further Inland Revenue limit on the lump sum itself. The maximum amount is calculated as 1.5 × final pensionable salary, provided that at least twenty years' service has been completed. This benefit is an anomaly in terms of benefits allowed under approved pension schemes, and so has been subject to gradual attack over the past few years.

There are various restrictions and limits which apply to cash sums payable from tax approved pension schemes. These are set by the Inland Revenue and are detailed in Appendix 2.

When designing the scheme it will be necessary to set the rate which is used to value the cash in pension terms under the scheme. The rate must accurately reflect the cost to the scheme of providing the pension, taking account of such factors as interest rates and guaranteed levels of increases to the pensions in payment. However the commutation rate can vary from time to time with fluctuating market interest rates unless it is guaranteed and enshrined in the Trust Deed and Rules. The basis of calculating commutation rates is therefore actuarially based.

The European Court of Justice has decided (*Neath* v *Hugh Steeper Ltd*) that commuted lump sums must be based on pensions which are based on the same pension age for men and women in respect of service after 17 May 1990 but the actuarial factors to calculate the lump sums can be based on the different life expectancies of the two sexes. As most, if not all, members take lump sum cash and reduced pension at retirement it may be beneficial to design the scheme in this way rather than provide a pension with the option to take cash. There can be funding advantages in doing this.

4.2.7 Early retirement

Schemes commonly provide for members to retire before reaching the normal pension date (NPD). This entails leaving service and having a pension payable immediately, instead of being deferred to normal pension date.

Early retirement may occur at the request of either the employee or the employer. Scheme designers need to consider carefully the terms under which early retirement may be granted to ensure that they are compatible with the employment policy of the employer. In particular, it is worth noting that in recent years early retirement has become a very important tool in normal employment patterns and redundancy exercises undertaken by employers. There is a considerable additional cost involved in providing pensions from a date earlier than the NPD. Consequently, an early retirement pension is frequently substantially reduced to ensure that there is a neutral cost effect on the scheme from its exercise. It is also common to allow alongside this discretion for the reduction to be adjusted or removed altogether at the request of the employer, although this is usually coupled with a requirement that the employer contributes the additional cost specifically identified as relating to that particular early retirement. It must be remembered that in any case the member's pension will be smaller because there have been fewer years' membership to accrue pension. The maximum benefit allowable is dictated by the Inland Revenue and will be affected by the reduced service he or she has completed.

Alternatively, early retirement can be forced by the poor health of the member. In this situation it is common for the scheme to provide a benefit greater than that earned up to the date of leaving the scheme, with the benefit quite often being calculated using a pensionable service figure that reflects in part or in whole the service which would have been achieved if the member had remained in employment to the NPD. In addition, the pension is frequently not reduced to take account of its early payment, as it would commonly be following voluntary early retirement. Once again, the maximum benefit allowable is dictated by the Inland Revenue, and in exceptional cases where a member is retiring because his or her life expectancy is then measured only in months, the Inland Revenue will allow the whole of the accrued value of the pension benefit under the scheme in respect of that member to be commuted for a cash sum (although the amount in excess of the normal tax-free cash amount will be subject to a deduction of tax at the rate of 20 per cent by the trustees).

Finally, the Finance Act 1989 introduced a new regime for early retirement pensions. Members affected by this regime are now able (providing the funding is available within the scheme) to receive a pension of a maximum of two-thirds of the final pensionable salary on early retirement from age 50 or later provided that they have completed at least twenty years' service by that date. This is an enhancement over the limits which apply under previous regimes and it is possible for members who are not subject to the 1989 Act regime to elect to be covered by it. However, such members would also then be subject to the earnings cap used to calculate maximum benefits.

4.2.8 Leaving service benefits

If a member leaves the service of his or her employer without qualifying for an early retirement pension, he or she will usually be entitled to the pension earned by service to the date of leaving, based upon the final pensionable salary at the date of leaving or a refund of his or her own contributions where scheme service is less than two years. This is a requirement imposed upon schemes by the preservation regulations first introduced by the Social Security Act 1973, and will be required effectively if a member has served at least two years in the employment whilst earning a pension from the scheme.

It is now also a requirement that pensions preserved in this way are revalued between the dates of leaving and retirement. The element of GMP (where applicable) has to be revalued according to one of the following methods:

1. A fixed rate of currently 7 per cent per annum compound for each complete tax year between the dates of leaving and state pension age.
2. A rate of revaluation known as 'Section 21 Orders' which is broadly equivalent to the annual rise in national average earnings.
3. A limited rate of revaluation of 5 per cent per annum compound or Section 21 Orders whichever is the smaller. If this is chosen then an additional sum is payable to the state (since the state will make up any balance) known as the limited revaluation premium.

A scheme may choose which of these methods it will use, but it must apply the chosen method consistently to all members at that time. The element of preserved pension which is in excess of the GMP has to be increased by set minimum revaluation rates which are announced annually. These are calculated as the lesser of RPI increases and 5 per cent per annum compound. The 1995 Pensions Act has introduced changes to contracting out of SERPS which will eliminate GMPs accruing after 1997 and the early leaver benefit will be calculated differently from the way shown above.

Attached to the preserved pension must be an option for the member to take the fair value of the preserved benefit (called a 'cash equivalent') to another scheme, whether it is the occupational pension scheme of a new employer or an individual arrangement. Individual arrangements may take the form of either a personal pension arrangement, or a statutory 'buy-out' policy effected with an insurance company, and commonly still referred to as 'Section 32' policies, after the original statutory section which first authorised their use.

Some schemes go further by providing that the early leaver benefit will have a value which is always as large as a multiple of the member's contributions often with an allowance for the investment return achieved over the period of membership – a 'money purchase underpin' or 'value for money' provision.

4.2.9 Death in service

It is usual for pension schemes to provide some form of benefit on the death of a member whilst in service. Benefits take the form of a lump sum and a spouse's or dependant's pension. The lump sum can be up to a multiple of four times the member's salary at the date of death, although lesser multiples are common for members of a lower status. The lump sum is usually written to be payable at the discretion of the trustees, to avoid its being assessed for inheritance tax. This lump sum is a large amount of money paid at an emotional time. Companies and trustees should recognise this and ensure that impartial professional advice is provided to the deceased's spouse or other beneficiary.

Pensions for spouses and dependants (including common law spouses and children) are also common. These can be expressed as a percentage of salary, payable as an annual pension. The maximum pension expressed in this way is an annual pension of four-ninths of the member's salary at the date of death. Again, lower multiples such as 25 per cent of salary are more common for lower-status employees.

Since the purpose of these benefits is to attempt to cover the late member's dependants' financial needs following the loss of the deceased's income, there are other common alternative methods of expressing the spouse's pension such as a percentage of the prospective pension (i.e. the pension which the member would expect to receive at retirement using his or her prospective service, based upon final pensionable salary at the date of death). This design is particularly successful in providing appropriate replacement income for dependants of younger members with little pensionable service completed before death.

Spouses' and dependants' pensions are, like lump sums, 'risk benefits', that is, the scheme may never be called upon to pay them. Larger schemes which have substantial assets building up in anticipation of the future retirement of members may be able to accept the risk without insurance other than possibly some stop loss or catastrophe insurance. Most smaller schemes, however, could not afford to carry this risk themselves and so such schemes frequently insure the risk.

4.2.10 Death after retirement

It is common to provide benefits for spouses of members who die in retirement. Once again, European law now requires widows and widowers to be treated equally in this respect. The maximum benefit which can be provided for a surviving spouse is two-thirds the maximum pension that could have been provided for the deceased member. Any increases to pensions in the course of payment which may apply to the member's pension may also be applied to increase the survivor's pension. However, once again it is rare for benefits to be provided at this maximum level, and a survivor's pension of 50 per cent is far more common.

In addition, in order to avoid the possible criticism, where a member dies soon after retirement, that he or she has failed to receive proper value for the pension earned over his service (and to which he or she may have contributed) it is usual to provide a guaranteed minimum period of payment of the pension. This is usually expressed in terms of a five-year guarantee, although a guarantee of up to ten years is permitted by the Inland Revenue. Guarantees of up to five years are commonly paid as a single lump sum, usually discounted appropriately to take account of the fact of early payment, possibly making allowance for anticipated pension increases. The survivor's pension may commence payment either on the member's death, or after the expiry of the appropriate guarantee period.

4.2.11 Member contributions

The question of whether members should contribute to their schemes is important and affects the overall benefit design. Some designers prefer to see members contributing, feeling that this will encourage them to value that pension scheme more highly, although others prefer schemes to be non-contributory on the part of members, fearing that members will be more critical if the benefits arising from the scheme did not match their expectations. In addition, non-contributory schemes may encourage employees to elect to join them, as opposed to effecting their own personal pension arrangements, particularly where those employees are young and have other financial commitments.

Whatever the decision on compulsory contributions, pension schemes must, by law, allow members to pay AVCs. A member may wish to pay

AVCs to improve the potential retirement benefits. This may be to enhance the benefits in respect of a short period of potential pensionable service, or alternatively may be to fund for the expectation of retiring early and needing to make up the reduction in the annual pension caused by the scheme's imposition of an early retirement reduction factor. The type of investment medium offered for AVCs received by the scheme, and also what form the benefit purchased by the AVCs will take must be considered. A small number of AVC schemes offer an additional final salary pension, but by far the most common benefit is a money purchase pool which is then applied at retirement to purchase additional pension or to buy additional increases in payment on the pension.

Member contributions are subject to Inland Revenue limits. A member may not contribute, in any one tax year, an amount in excess of 15 per cent of his total taxable remuneration (up to the earnings cap in the case of a member subject to the regulatory regime introduced by the Finance Act 1989). This limit applies to the aggregate of all contributions by the employee to all schemes connected with that employment and so would include AVCs to the scheme, and also contributions to any FSAVC scheme.

If, when the benefits come to be payable, it becomes apparent that AVCs have created a fund which is too large to secure benefits within Inland Revenue limits, it is now possible for the accumulated AVC funds to be returned to the member, subject to a tax deduction. The tax payable is 35 per cent for basic-rate tax-payers, with an additional rate payable by higher-rate tax-payers. The rules relating to the calculation and refund of excessive AVCs are complicated and expert advice is needed to apply them.

4.3 The defined contribution scheme

Many of the elements of scheme design identified above in respect of defined benefit schemes also apply to defined contribution schemes. In particular, the questions of eligibility, normal retirement date, death benefits and contributions need to receive a similar degree of consideration. Clearly, however, questions of pension amounts, whether at normal, early or late retirement are not applicable, since amounts of benefit are by definition dependent upon the contributions made to the scheme and the investment return thereon.

It must be remembered that the limits set by the Inland Revenue and identified variously above also apply to benefits arising from defined contribution occupational schemes. Consequently, contribution levels must be set at a realistic level having regard to the likely levels of benefits which they will secure at retirement or leaving.

The design will concentrate more on the level of contributions and whether they should in some way reflect the member's age and service period with the company. It is not uncommon to start with a target pension and determine the contribution rate required to achieve this benefit.

4.4 Flexible benefits

The changing circumstances of many employees can for some companies make the design of suitable pension schemes very difficult. They are too often targeted to provide reasonable benefits for the average employee, but no such person exists. To counter the problem encountered by the early leaver many final salary schemes introduced a 'money purchase underpin' to ensure that the value of a member's benefits was always as large as a multiple of the member's contributions (with interest). This was aimed particularly at that group of members who leave service after a short period of years.

A far larger extension of this principle is the concept of flexible benefits where an individual is provided with an allowance to spend on a range of employee benefits offered by the employer. There is certainly a growing concern amongst many employers at the increasing costs of providing employee benefits. This had led to pressures to provide benefits to employees which provide maximum value from the employee's perspective – obviously at minimum cost to the employer. The individual is able to choose the benefits that are perceived to be of most value. The allowance available to an individual, the costs of purchasing benefits and rules for making selections are governed by the employer. Fitting pension provision into a flexible benefits programme needs careful attention. Certain basic core pension benefits would be required but the advantage for the employee is the ability to tailor the remaining provision to suit current and anticipated needs. Flexible benefits is a concept which embraces all employee benefits including such items as cars, holiday and welfare as well as pensions and so detailed study is outside the scope of this book.

4.5 Conclusion

Whatever the type of pension scheme you decide on give some thought to the flexibility and adaptability of the scheme to your changing business needs. Clearly you do not want to be undertaking major reviews of your pension scheme too frequently – either as a consequence of legislation or changing business practice. Designing a scheme with the future in mind takes time but is well worth the effort.

Checklist 4   Designing the scheme

Company issues
- changing employment patterns – company
- changing employment patterns – industry
- employee sex and service profile
- turnover of workforce
- target retirement income/allowance for state benefits
- target cost
- industry and competitor comparisons

Employee needs
- attitude survey
- flexibility and portability
- security and risk
- ease of understanding
- flexible benefits

Benefits
- defined benefit/defined contribution
- eligibility
- pension age
- retirement pension and pensionable pay
- increases to pensions in payment
- early retirement and ill-health retirement
- cash at retirement
- spouses' pensions
- life assurance
- leaving service benefits
- contracted-out or not
- benefits for those who do not join
- members' contributions

5 Balance of powers

5.1 Taking decisions

The modern occupational pension scheme is a highly complex animal which needs to be efficiently and effectively managed (over a long period of time – potentially even in perpetuity). Like the company itself it needs to have sufficient built-in flexibility to enable it to function in constantly changing social, economic and legislative environments. Decisions need to be made regularly about matters from investment and funding levels through to the provision of discretionary benefits for members in hardship. Trustees will need to be appointed, and then replaced when they no longer wish to continue or are no longer suitable to fill the post. Finally the whole basis of the scheme itself may need to be altered in the light of changes in the fiscal or legal regimes governing schemes, and proposed changes in legislation such as the 1995 Pensions Act or because of changes in the needs of the company sponsoring the scheme.

This chapter concentrates on current legislation and practice and from time to time refers the reader to Chapter 12 where the implications of proposed legislation are considered.

It is important to determine from the outset the areas where decisions will be necessary and to identify which of the various parties connected with the scheme will be involved in taking each of them. It should be regarded as part of the scheme design. However, in view of the fact that under trust law the trustees are responsible for the proper running of the trust and that liability is personal to them, the choice is usually between the trustees and the company, which has a continuing interest in the scheme both through its ongoing financial liability and because the whole purpose of the scheme is to provide retirement and other relevant benefits for its workforce.

The allocation of powers between these two parties is of paramount importance. Each of them will have different priorities to consider when exercising those powers – priorities which may well conflict with one another (although as we shall see later in this chapter the law has imposed some restrictions on the extent to which trustees and non-trustees may exercise their powers for their own benefit alone). The issues should also be considered from the outset when planning the scheme, since although nearly every scheme will have a specific power to amend aspects of it, such amendments become more difficult to make once there are members who have built up rights under it. In addition, where the proposal is to remove a power granted originally to the trustees, and to give it instead to the company, and the power of amendment is given jointly to the company and the trustees, it may be difficult for the trustees to justify agreeing to give up the power. Even where (unusually) the trustees are granted no say in any proposed amendments, trust law has a basic antipathy towards a party who sets up a trust exercising powers subsequently to increase its control over the trust.

Despite its importance this area is one which is frequently glossed-over in the rush to set up a new scheme. Many of the powers and duties may be legitimately given to one of several parties, or even shared, and the decision as to the distribution of powers may vary according to the circumstances of the particular scheme and the parties to it. Many companies, when setting up a scheme, will spend long hours agonising over the benefit basis, the investment media and the cost of actuarial advice, but will leave to 'the experts' the choice over how the trustees are appointed, who retains and instructs the actuary, or who makes rule amendments. After all, who wants to consider the winding-up provisions before the scheme has even been established? And yet, if the scheme winds up with assets in excess of its liabilities (perhaps voluntarily as a result of a corporate re-organisation with the company wishing to replace the old scheme with a new one more suited to its changed structure and corporate needs), the question of what to do with that surplus, and the identity of the party or parties who will ultimately decide, may become crucial. It is not unheard of for a company, following a corporate merger, to conclude that it needs one combined pension scheme for all its employees, in place of the two or more existing schemes set up pre-merger by each of the companies. Many companies in that position, with schemes in surplus, have then discovered to their horror that on wind-up the rules give the trustees the sole right to decide on the use of such surplus, and that the incumbent trustees wish to spend all of the surplus on improving the benefits of members, instead of holding some in reserve against future liabilities, or in helping the company with its re-organisation expenses by allowing it to have a contribution holiday. The changes in the 1995 Pensions Act have impact in this respect and are considered in Chapter 12.

Schemes bought from insurance companies as packages will generally not offer any flexibility in this area. It is therefore important, when considering the package on offer, to look at the documents which the insurer is proposing to use, and to consider the balance of powers between the parties. If it does not fit the company's requirements, then consideration should be given to using a different insurance company's package, or perhaps if the rest of the package is acceptable, to commission a firm of solicitors or specialist consultants to draft documents which contain acceptable provisions. Such a course of action will, of course, incur additional charges, since the insurance company's package costs will already contain an element for documentation. However, a cheaper compromise may be possible by, for instance, instructing the solicitors to draft the trust deed containing the powers and duties of the trustees, and appending the insurance company's standard rules to it.

Companies setting up a self-administered scheme will be able to instruct their advisers from the outset on the balance of powers issue (subject to legal and other overriding constraints). Either way this area is of great importance and the purpose of this chapter is to help you identify the issues and decide on the right balance for your schemes. The 1995 Pensions Act (see Chapter 12) gives more powers to trustees, which means you should be even more vigilant in allocating the remaining powers between company and trustees and ensuring you have a detailed understanding of the powers vested in the company and trustees.

5.2 Parties and powers

5.2.1 The trust

Before considering powers and their balance in detail, it is necessary first to understand the legal basis governing schemes, the parties involved and their roles in relation to the scheme.

Company-sponsored pension schemes must be set up under trust if they are to obtain formal approval (and thereby concessionary tax treatment) from the Inland Revenue. Although the basic concept of a trust is simple, this area of law has developed into a highly complex subject since its medieval beginnings. In its simplest form the trust is an arrangement whereby one party (the settlor) gives property to another (the trustee) to hold for the benefit of a third party (the beneficiary). The trustee is the legal owner of the property transferred, but the terms of the trust override the trustee's own personal interest and provide that he or she is only holding the property on behalf of the beneficiary. Translated into pension scheme terms, the settlor is the company, the trustee is the person or persons appointed to hold that position, and the beneficiary is the scheme member and any dependant entitled to a benefit from the scheme on the death of the member.

The use of a trust for a funded pension scheme enables assets to be set aside for the benefit of beneficiaries at some future date while being beyond the reach of the company and its creditors. The further attraction to the Inland Revenue is that the monies paid out of the employer's business cease to be under the employer's control as beneficial owner, thereby preventing the company (except in well-defined circumstances) from having access to a pool of tax-free funds for corporate purposes.

This is a pension scheme in its simplest form. In practice, however, a number of factors may complicate the position and, to the layman, blur the straightforward distinctions between the various parties and their duties. Such complications usually arise out of situations where one individual or organisation fulfils more than one of the three roles described. The problem is particularly acute where the company is also the trustee – a common situation in package schemes, but certainly not considered to be good practice. In addition, there are frequently powers reserved to the employer by the scheme's documents which it must nevertheless exercise in a particular way or subject to particular conditions. This is dealt with in more detail later in this chapter.

5.2.2 The parties

Company

The company is the party which establishes the scheme and pays for most or all of the benefits and usually the running costs. There is no obligation on a company to set up a pension scheme for its employees, but motives for doing so range from paternalism through to the purely commercial. As the settlor under the trust, the company has the power to set up the initial benefit structure and also to detail the terms of the trust itself. It will appoint the first trustees and will normally retain the right to dismiss and appoint trustees subsequently (but see section 12.5). Unlike the settlors of the conventional family trusts, it usually retains for itself some powers to amend the scheme, and ultimately to terminate it. It reserves such a right because it has a legitimate continuing interest in the scheme primarily because of the contributions which it is committed to making. In addition, a pension scheme is a very long-term undertaking and, if the business continues, may last in perpetuity. Whatever the motives involved in setting up the scheme initially, and those which shaped its original form, the passage of time will almost certainly render aspects of the initial benefit structure obsolete in due course. The company is often the single body best placed to ascertain whether changes need to be made to the pension scheme, although the trustees will often have relevant knowledge which should be taken into account. For this reason the power of amendment is commonly shared with the trustees (see below).

Trustees

Trustees are appointed to run the scheme for the benefit of the beneficiaries. They must do so in accordance with both the specific provisions in their governing trust documents, and any overriding legal requirements such as trust law and the specific requirements of the Inland Revenue and the OPB, all of whose regulations are so numerous and complex that specific reference to all of them in the scheme's documentation is simply not possible. Trustees have a duty to act fairly towards all of the beneficiaries under the scheme, and also to ensure that scheme assets are properly and safely managed and that the scheme is administered in the terms of its documents. They may employ agents to do the day-to-day work for them, but they will still retain personal liability for the acts of their agents. Trustees should remember that they are not representatives of the workforce charged with negotiating scheme improvements with the company, neither are they representatives of the company charged with helping company profits at the expense of beneficiaries.

Members and other beneficiaries

These, the past and present employees of the company and their dependants, are the ultimate parties to benefit from the scheme. Their rights and benefits are determined in accordance with the scheme documents, subject to any overriding legal provisions. Members will have their right to benefit specifically described in the scheme's rules, but some dependants may only have the right to be considered for a benefit, at the trustees' discretion. An example is a lump sum payable on a member's death, which will be paid to a party selected by the trustees from a defined class of possible beneficiaries. The member may nominate his or her choice of beneficiary, but the decision is that of the trustees alone. This is a technical device both to allow rapid payment of the benefit and to avoid its assessment to inheritance tax.

As beneficiaries under a trust, members have the right to bring an action against the trustees to compensate them for any loss incurred as a result of the trustees' acts or omissions. It is important to stress that the beneficiaries' interest in the scheme is itself restricted to that set out under the scheme's documents. This sometimes causes difficulty in circumstances where the documents provide for some benefits to be paid or not at the discretion of the trustees. Most common is the situation where a scheme provides that pensions in payment will not be automatically increased, but that the trustees have discretion to award increases to pensioners where they consider that they have sufficient assets in hand and that it is reasonable to apply those assets in that way. The use by the trustees of this discretion for a few consecutive years may create an expectation amongst the membership that such increases will continue in the future. However, this expectation is not a right and the members will still have no right to compel trustees to continue awarding such increases where the trustees consider it inappropriate to do so.

Managing committee

This kind of committee is most commonly found in larger companies with substantial self-administered pension schemes. Its role is usually that of liaison between members, trustees and the company. It provides a means by which ideas, comments and other information can be collated, sifted and presented to the other parties. It may oversee the day-to-day administration of the scheme. However, a committee and its members are not normally parties to the trust and their powers and duties should not be set out in the scheme's documents. Consequently they do not play a direct role in respect of the rest of this chapter.

Professional advisers

These are individuals or bodies to whom powers or responsibilities are delegated, and who are not parties with primary responsibilities set out in the scheme's documents, unless they are also appointed as trustees, which is now restricted under the 1995 Pensions Act (see Chapter 12). Their role may be defined in the trust deed (for example, the deed will usually specify that an actuary shall be appointed to advise on the funding position of the scheme) but their responsibility will be to the trustees and/or to the company, rather than to the trust itself. The distinction is important because the advisers' terms of appointment will be set by the trustees and/or the company, rather than by the deed or trust law, and the trustees will remain responsible to the trust (and therefore the beneficiaries) for ensuring that the advisers' duties are properly discharged. Consequently the advisers are not parties to the trust as such and their powers and duties do not need to be considered in a discussion of the balance of powers between parties to the scheme.

Thus we can clearly see the likely roles of each of the parties to the scheme, and the basis upon which any liability attached to those roles is enforceable. This leads to the conclusion that the two parties that are most likely to be directly responsible to the scheme (and therefore subject to enforcement measures brought by scheme beneficiaries) are the company and the trustees. Of all the parties responsible for running the scheme, it is they who have the greatest personal interests to protect. Any question of the balance of powers therefore comes down to a comparison between those of the company and the trustees.

The next step therefore is to examine the powers which are commonly required to be exercised in respect of company schemes, and which must be allocated between the trustees and the company.

5.2.3 The powers

Appointment and removal of trustees

This is most commonly given to the company, although some schemes have self-perpetuating trustee bodies. Generally trustees can be corporate bodies or individuals, subject only to their not being minors, of unsound mind, or undischarged bankrupts. There are also restrictions on the appointment of trustees living overseas. Although the power to change trustees cannot be exercised for selfish motives (see below) there still in practice remains considerable scope for a company retaining the power to influence the 'flavour' of the trustee board and therefore its attitude towards the interests of the company.

The 1995 Pensions Act requires that one-third of the trustees is elected by the members of the scheme and that they could only subsequently be removed by a unanimous decision from the remaining trustees (see Chapter 12).

Trustees' decision-making processes

Trustees' decision-making processes, the frequency and conduct of meetings and the question of whether matters can be decided by majority, are matters usually left for the trustees themselves to decide although they are increasingly subject to legislative requirements and have little effect on the balance between the parties.

Investment decisions

In defined benefits 'balance of cost' schemes the company clearly has a strong interest in the scheme's investment performance. Day-to-day investment decisions are, however, usually delegated to specialist investment managers, to avoid the need for the trustees or the company to register with a statutory regulatory organisation (SRO) under the Financial Services Act 1986. The responsibility for investments is usually given to the trustees (it sits more naturally with their legal duties) but the company may exercise influence through having an input in the choice of the investment manager.

Delegation of duties

The delegation of duties, the appointment of officers and the obtaining of professional advice are usually given to the trustees. The company may have a legitimate interest, however, on cost grounds.

Appointment of the actuary and the right to receive actuarial report

Whilst it is quite normal for the actuary to work for both the company and the trustees, there will be occasions when a conflict of interest between those parties will arise and the actuary will need to decide for whom he or she is working. Therefore a clear statement on this point should be contained in the scheme documents. The 1995 Pensions Act gives trustees the sole responsibility for appointing the actuary and auditors in particular.

The payment of scheme expenses

This is not generally an important issue in practice, since the company will probably pay the expenses whether directly or indirectly through an adjustment of the funding rate (in a defined benefit scheme). Note, however, that expenses cannot be paid directly out of the fund unless the rules specifically allow.

   If the expenses are to be paid out of the fund, VAT will not be recoverable unless the trustees are VAT registered.

Decisions on matters of doubt and settlement of disputes

Usually the interpretation of the scheme provisions is left to the trustees and will be for the future (see Chapter 12). Failure to allocate this responsibility effectively can lead to the need for expensive legal assistance at an earlier point than is necessary.

The inclusion of new employers

Since this has the potential to affect matters with which both the company and the trustees are concerned, the agreement of both parties is commonly required.

Application of the fund on cessation of participation of an employer or following the cessation of the scheme itself

Schemes are divided on whether these powers more correctly belong to the company or to the trustees. The issue at stake is, of course, who controls any surplus identified at that point, since these are occasions when a positive decision about the application of any accrued surplus must be taken. Some older schemes (mainly those set up under packages by insurance companies) are dangerously unclear on this point, apparently relying on an allocation of assets having been made through the underlying policy. Some of those schemes have been converted to a self-administered basis without clarification of this power, leaving the schemes open to expensive litigation and delay to clarify the point.

The tendency now is to share the power between the company and trustees, or to give it to the company alone (although this is clearly a fiduciary power – see later in this chapter – which restricts the company's ability to exercise it in a purely selfish manner). However, under the 1995 Pensions Act the control of surplus in the event of the scheme ceasing will be in the hands solely of the trustees.

The award of discretionary benefits

The award of discretionary benefits and dealing with surpluses and deficits in assets in an on-going scheme are again powers which have ramifications for both the trustees and the company, and for that reason they are commonly shared. Some schemes do grant them entirely to the company but again they are fiduciary powers with the effects that implies.

Scheme amendments

This power is clearly one of the most important contained in a scheme. Its inclusion is vital to enable changes to be made to keep the scheme relevant to the purpose for which it exists, and its significance lies in its potential ability to change radically most other aspects of the scheme. However, it is not necessarily an open-ended power. Traditionally trust law has a dislike of powers to amend trusts once they have been established, and will interpret any such power literally. If the power does not allow the amendment being proposed, then the amendment cannot be made. Furthermore, certain matters are deemed by many to be incapable of being changed other than by overriding legislation. These include the order of priority given to benefits when a scheme is wound up.

However, the party in whose hands this power is placed is still in a very powerful position in respect of the scheme. For all these reasons it is common to share the power jointly between the company and the trustees, and sometimes its exercise in certain circumstances will require the written consent of scheme members who are directly affected by the proposed change.

Government proposals suggest further restrictions in this area particularly to avoid the worsening of member's accrued rights (see Chapter 12).

Receipt and payment of transfer values

Again, this power is generally shared, since it affects both the company's and the trustees' interests.

Decision on whether to buy out pensions in payment

Many larger self-administered schemes pay pension instalments out of their fund, rather than purchasing an annuity from an insurance company. It is often a difficult equation to balance the administration cost of paying the pension direct against the immediate cost of paying a premium to an insurance company based on its actuary's assessment of the annuitant's potential life expectancy and the return the insurer will be able to obtain on its investment of that premium. Clearly this has implications for both the company and the trustees, although the power is commonly only given to the latter party because they can usually be relied upon to take a reasonable decision to minimise costs.

Special terms and late-joining employees

The inclusion of employees to membership on special terms and consideration of employees who apply later to join have implications for the company in its roles as employer and paymaster, the trustees in their role of custodian of the fund and the accrued interests of existing members. Consequently it is usual for both parties to have to agree to the inclusion of a member on special terms or after expiry of the normal joining time, with the trustees having the right to call for an additional contribution from the employer if necessary.

The level of employer contributions

This is clearly a very contentious area and links in with the power to appoint the actuary (see above). It goes to the heart of the funding issue, particularly in a 'balance of cost' defined benefit scheme. However, it is more usual to place the immediate duty of the trustees to see that the liabilities are properly covered and to ensure that the proposed minimum solvency levels are satisfied (see Chapter 12) above the interest of the company. Well-designed schemes should have a provision allowing the company to terminate its liability to continue to contribute to the scheme in future, which will offer some safeguard against costs running out of control.

Members' options

The granting of options to members such as early or late retirement, commutation, optional dependants' pensions, etc., and the disposal of lump sum death benefits are powers which are usually costed so that they have a neutral effect on scheme funding. They are therefore usually given solely to the trustees to exercise as they see fit for the benefit of the appropriate beneficiaries.

5.3 Getting the balance right

The main point to note from the outset is that there is no one 'ideal' balance for all schemes or all sponsoring companies. Similarly there is no one ideal method of achieving a given balance between the parties. It should be stressed that not following the norm in the allocation of a power to a party is not necessarily wrong. It is the overall balance which is the important factor. For example, a defined benefit scheme may provide that the inclusion of new employers is at the sole discretion of the company, but that the setting of a contribution rate to fund the benefits of its employees is the responsibility of the trustees, so that an employer company or group cannot use its power to dilute the fund already built up for the benefit of existing employees. Such a 'balancing' power given to trustees may be particularly useful to avoid an 'asset stripping' company acquiring the employer company in a hostile takeover and gaining the benefit of a surplus in the scheme by putting its own employees in and using the surplus to gain a temporary break from the need to contribute to its pension arrangements.

This 'balance' may then be upset by a provision in the same scheme which gives the company sole right to appoint and dismiss the majority of trustees. Although a company may not exercise such a power in a capricious manner, and trustees, once appointed, must perform their duties for the sole benefit of the beneficiaries, these are nevertheless vague concepts which may be difficult to enforce in practice. The view of one set of trustees as to a 'proper' contribution rate, and therefore funding level, may differ radically from another and yet there may be room for both views to be held legally. In this way the company may manipulate the funding level of the scheme.

But who is to say what is the correct balance? After all, in a defined benefit scheme the company does retain a legitimate interest in the funding level because as a company it will not want to see an excessively large amount of capital unnecessarily being tied up in a pension scheme where that capital is, effectively, beyond its reach and control.

This question of balance forms one of the cornerstones of the Goode Committee's Report, the White Paper and the 1995 Pensions Act. Several of the proposals were designed to curb the potential for an unscrupulous company or other party to manipulate a pension scheme to the detriment of the interests of the beneficiaries. It is a useful reminder that there may be restrictions on the allocation and use of powers by particular parties – but mainly companies – in the future.

Meanwhile the judiciary has been steadily eroding the freedom of companies to exercise in a particular way powers which may be given to them. A recent line of cases, for example, has established the principle that certain powers, even when legitimately given to (or retained by) a company, must be exercised primarily for the benefit of beneficiaries. These 'fiduciary' powers, as they are known, include the power to determine how surplus assets are applied, how scheme provisions may be amended, and may possibly also affect the exercise of the power to appoint and remove trustees. The limits of the principle have yet to be determined, and potentially may be expanded to cover every power retained by a company in respect of a scheme.

Consequently even though scheme designers may put in a particular balance, it may in practice be tilted by the subsequent intervention of the law. Nevertheless this does not detract from the need to consider the issues carefully when designing schemes. A design which hands over too much control to trustees may subsequently have catastrophic effects on the viability of the company – and with the costs associated with providing 'final salary' pensions, catastrophes can result from costs running out of control and the company finding itself liable to pick up the bill for costs already incurred but which may not have become apparent at the time they arose. On the other hand, too much power in the hands of the company might undermine scheme members' confidence or make it too easy for the company – perhaps under new management – to misuse the pension fund.

5.4 Conclusion

The perceived right balance for any particular scheme will depend largely on the standpoint of the particular company. This book cannot recommend an 'ideal' balance as this is up to scheme designers and those instructing them. The best we can do is to counsel careful consideration of the points identified in this chapter.

Checklist 5   Balance of powers

- appointment of trustees
- frequency of trustees' meetings
- majority decisions
- settlement of disputes
- delegation of duties

- professional advisers
- appointment of actuary
- appointment of auditor

- scheme expenses
- treatment of surplus
- discretionary benefits
- employer contributions

- inclusion of new employers
- inclusion of employees on special terms
- benefit options
- transfer values – receipt and payment
- buying out pensions

- cessation of participating employer
- cessation of scheme

C The scheme in operation

If benefits are not paid on time, members become disillusioned and lose faith. Continually achieving a poor investment return reduces security for accrued benefits and increases future costs. Being a professionally cautious person, the actuary may encourage a funding strategy which syphons funds away from the company and shareholders and into the pension scheme. It is therefore of more than passing interest to the company that it understands how the scheme operates and achieves value for money from its contributions to the scheme. This section considers the major aspects of running the scheme and what can be done to monitor progress and achieve objectives.

6 Day-to-day administration

Every pension arrangement needs some day-to-day administration. If the scheme is of the 'insured' variety, this is usually undertaken by the insurance company concerned as part of the 'package'. Where there is no such insurer involved, the trustees or the company will have to arrange administration separately, and may even go so far as to establish a dedicated pensions administration team employed and managed by the company. Either way, the company will be involved, at least to the extent of providing information from time to time to the administrator, and probably in providing a channel of communication between the administrator, the trustees and the member.

Good administration is vital and with the ever-increasing complexity of pension schemes and their administration, it is now almost universal for the administration to be either partly or fully computerised. The administrative service is the medium by which the membership sees at first hand what the scheme is about, so getting it right is vital.

This chapter covers the main day-to-day administrative tasks involving the collection and payment of contributions, the calculation and payment of benefits, record keeping and communication with members.

6.1 Contributions

The collection of contributions, whether employers' or (where applicable) employees', is normally handled by the payroll department of the employer. In practice contributions are often collected on behalf of the trustees directly from the employer by the investment manager or the insurance company involved. This saves on administrative work and means that the money starts earning a return for the fund immediately – provided both company and members' contributions are deducted and paid on time, in accordance with the trustees' instructions.

In many cases the contributions will be invested with an insurance company or investment manager who will allocate the money to purchase units in a managed fund. Some fund managers only operate on a dealing date once each month and it is vital that the contributions are received in advance of this date so that they do not sit around waiting to be invested. If the scheme is of the contracted-out money purchase (COMP) variety, the

NI rebate needs to be invested along with the other contributions on a monthly basis, as described in Chapter 2.

Out of the employer contribution rate there may also be an allowance for payment of expenses such as premiums for life assurance or fees to advisers of the scheme. Alternatively these may be paid by the employer in addition to the pension scheme contributions. They may even be paid out of the fund assets.

The collection and investment of pension scheme contributions should not be an onerous task. Providing that the systems are set up within the payroll and accounts department the monthly tasks should run smoothly but they must be checked from time to time as in this area procedures can fall into disrepair and misunderstandings arise.

6.2 Benefits

The object of a pension scheme is, of course, to pay out benefits. Therefore the setting up of efficient procedures for dealing with members' benefits on retirement or death is vital to the operation of the scheme. Many members will leave the scheme prior to the normal pension age and the procedures concerning this event are the most complicated. Unfortunately some members will die before retirement. If the scheme is wholly insured the insurers provide much of the information needed by the employer and trustees as and when their members become entitled to receive benefits.

For those schemes that are not receiving such a service this section covers the procedures to follow for all of the possible events that can occur during a member's period of membership.

6.2.1 Early leavers

The benefits paid to an early leaver will be determined by the scheme rules. They are affected by factors such as whether or not the member contributed, whether the member is leaving voluntarily, whether the scheme is contracted-out and whether the member has completed more than two years' qualifying service (see below). In most cases the administrator will be notified by the personnel department of a member's impending departure. At this stage the appropriate final remuneration details as well as any contributions or NI contracted-out details since the last scheme renewal date should also be provided. If a member has been making AVCs it is important to include these details in any calculations.

Where a member has completed less than two years' qualifying service (as defined in the preservation requirements contained in the Social Security Act 1973), he or she may be entitled only to a refund of his or her own contributions either with or without interest added. If the scheme is contracted-out the trustees will have to repay an amount in respect of the joint savings on NI contributions known as the contributions equivalent premium (CEP) to the DSS to re-instate the member into SERPS. The employee's portion of the saving is known as the certified amount and this is deducted from the gross contribution refund made to him or her. The balance is subject to a tax charge at 20 per cent which is normally deducted before payment. In some cases the rules may also give the additional option of a preserved pension and/or a transfer to another arrangement.

Where the member has completed more than two years' qualifying service, he or she will have a right to a preserved benefit which will be determined under the rules of the scheme. Where the scheme is contracted-out at least part of the benefit arising must take the form of a GMP or a pension purchased by the protected rights fund and will be subject to special treatment which must be observed. In addition, a deceased's spouse is also entitled to a GMP related to the member's GMP or protected rights. For a widower this element is limited to benefit applicable to service since April 1988.

Under a defined benefits scheme the employer is required to increase the preserved pension between the date of leaving and retirement. If the benefit includes a GMP element then this must be revalued by the method in operation for the scheme which is either fixed or limited rate revaluation or revaluation in accordance with Section 21 Orders. The increases on any pension in excess of the GMP will depend on the member's date of leaving. If the member left between 1 January 1986 and 31 December 1990 only the excess in respect of service after 1 January 1985 needs to be revalued (although the scheme may be more generous). If the member left service on or after 1 January 1991, all of the preserved pension in excess of the GMP must be revalued. Revaluation is in accordance with published rates calculated in line with the rise in the RPI but limited to a maximum of 5 per cent per annum compound. This statutory revaluation does not apply to money purchase benefits.

6.2.2 Transfers: out

A member who leaves on or after 1 January 1986 with a right to a preserved pension has as an alternative the right (to be exercised no later than one year before the NPD) to move the cash equivalent of his or her preserved benefits to another arrangement. This is calculated as at the later of the date of leaving or the date of his or her written request to the trustees for a transfer value to be paid. This cash equivalent must be calculated and verified in the manner approved by a qualified actuary who must certify that the methods are consistent with Guidance Note 11 issued jointly by the Institute and Faculty of Actuaries.

As long as the receiving arrangement satisfies prescribed requirements the transferring scheme is fully discharged of all its liabilities when the transfer is paid. Generally if the transfer is to another occupational pension scheme, the receiving scheme must certify that it is an approved scheme and that the member has entered employment with an employer who is a contributor to it. If the member wishes to transfer to a buy-out policy, commonly known as a 'Section 32', the insurance company concerned must certify that it is authorised to carry on ordinary long-term insurance business in the United Kingdom and that it will apply the cash equivalent to provide benefits under an approved Inland Revenue policy. Finally the member may wish to transfer to a personal pension arrangement and in this case the provider must certify that the personal pension scheme is approved by the Inland Revenue.

It should also be mentioned that under the Social Security Act 1986 employees were given the right to leave their occupational pension scheme any time after 6 April 1988 without leaving company service. Where an employee decides to 'opt-out' he or she should usually be asked to complete a form notifying the trustees of his or her decision. This form would include a statement that the member understands the implications of the decision. This is particularly important where the member loses cover for life assurance. If the member is giving up spouse's benefits it may be beneficial to obtain the spouse's confirmation as well. However, the member has a statutory right and can insist on the 'opt-out' without these 'comforts' for the trustees. There may also be restrictions on him or her rejoining the scheme at a future date. The benefits in such a case will depend on the scheme rules and the service completed but all employees have a statutory right to transfer to another arrangement that part of their entitlement earned after 6 April 1988.

6.2.3 Transfers: in

Whilst mentioning transfers out it is, of course, important to remember the reverse side which is transfer in to the scheme. When a new employee joins the scheme he or she may have benefits in a previous employer's scheme, a personal pension policy or a free-standing AVC policy. The administrators of the new scheme will need to establish details of the previous arrangement, details of the benefit preserved, the transfer value available and contracted-out information (if applicable). In addition the administrators will need to know the period of qualifying service in the previous arrangement, the maximum cash lump sum and the Inland Revenue maximum rules that apply in the old scheme. This will then enable them to calculate the benefit that could be secured by the transfer value in their scheme. This may be expressed as a money purchase value, as a notional additional number of years of service or as a fixed pension. However, it is not a requirement that trustees accept transfers in.

6.2.4 Retirement: normal

Retirement at the NPD is becoming less common, but where the situation does arise there is plenty of time for both the employer and the employee to supply information and make decisions prior to the event. The member should be notified at least eight weeks before normal pension age of the options available. This will usually be either a full pension or a tax free cash lump sum together with a reduced pension. In both cases the spouse's pension payable on death after retirement will be quoted. In some cases pension benefits are based on a final remuneration figure which cannot be determined until the actual date of leaving. However, the member should still be in a position to indicate the type of benefit he or she wishes to receive. In some cases a fund will pay the pension instalments itself but in others the pension will be bought out in the form of an annuity with an insurance company. Either way there will be paperwork for the member to complete in respect of bank or building society details for the receipt of the regular pension instalments. The pension will be taxed in the same way as ordinary salary. If a member has elected to receive the tax-free cash sum this should be paid at or immediately after retirement. In some cases this can include proceeds from AVCs and it may be necessary for a separate cheque to be forwarded in respect of that amount.

Where the pension value of a member's total benefits under the scheme is less than a specified amount (currently £260 per annum) the benefits are regarded by the Inland Revenue as trivial and can be paid wholly in cash. If the lump sum exceeds the Inland Revenue maximum applicable to that member the excess is taxable at 20 per cent. This tax is payable by the scheme but the scheme rules may allow the trustees to deduct it from the payment to the member.

6.2.5 Retirement: early

In many cases, the member will take the initiative by requesting details of the benefits payable on early retirement. The scheme rules will usually require the consent of both the employer and the trustees to any proposed early retirement, so that must be obtained first. The figures are then calculated in accordance with the scheme rules and generally include a reduction for early payment. If early retirement is caused by ill-health or possibly redundancy, it is likely that benefits will be augmented either in line with the rules or at the discretion of the trustees. Ill-health must follow the Inland Revenue definition which is 'physical or mental deterioration which is enough to prevent the individual from following his normal occupation, or which seriously impairs his earning capacity'. In the case of serious ill-health where life expectancy can be measured in months, the member may fully commute the pension for cash, subject to the tax charge mentioned in the preceding paragraph.

6.2.6 Retirement: late

If the member wishes to continue in employment after the NPD he or she will normally defer receipt of benefits until actual retirement (although it is possible to take the benefits from the NPD and scheme rules will often give the option). Once again, the consent of the employer and/or the trustees may be required by the rules. In addition, regardless of the scheme rules, the employer's consent will usually be needed in terms of the employment relationship. If the member is subject to an Inland Revenue approval regime introduced before 1989, the pension or cash sum or both may be taken at the normal pension age even though retirement is deferred. In cases of late retirement the benefits are either increased by a mathematical factor or the period of service after the NPD earns additional benefits as if the service were performed before the NPD.

6.2.7 Pension increases

The increases to pensions once in payment will depend both on whether or not the scheme is contracted-out and the type of scheme. Contracted-out final salary schemes have to increase the GMP in relation to service from 6 April 1988 by 3 per cent a year (or RPI if less). The state increases GMPs each year in relation to service before 6 April 1988 in line with the RPI. It does the same for GMPs earned from 6 April 1988, but excluding the first 3 per cent which is the scheme's responsibility.

In contracted-out money purchase schemes the state is responsible for increasing the notional GMP secured by the protected rights fund from age 60 onwards by the amount each year by which the RPI increase exceeds 3 per cent. The pension actually secured by contributions to the scheme must be increased by the scheme in line with increases in the RPI up to a maximum of 3 per cent.

For defined benefit schemes the Social Security Act 1990 introduced new legislation that requires the scheme to increase the excess over the GMP once in payment in line with RPI up to a maximum of 5 per cent per annum compound. This is known colloquially as limited price indexation (LPI). The effective date of legislation had still to be announced at the time of writing but will be known as A-day. From this date onwards the part of the pension built up on service from A-day must be increased by LPI. This legislation does not apply to service before A-day, to money purchase schemes or to those retiring before A-day. The 1995 Pensions Act has now proposed that A-day be set for April 1997.

At present, LPI has to be introduced in respect of all accrued benefits (including pensions in payment) before any surplus can be paid to the company.

6.2.8 Death benefits

The payment of death benefits, particularly arising from the death of a member in service, is an area where it is particularly important to have procedures in place to ensure swift completion of documentation and prompt payment of benefits.

For members who die in service before the NPD the benefits that arise are normally insured. In particular it is common for the lump sum, usually expressed as a multiple of salary, to be covered by insurance. However any spouse's and/or children's pensions may also be insured. Where an insurance company is involved, the standard form will need to be completed and forwarded together with the death certificate. If the member was contracted-out and paying AVCs this information also needs to be collected. In a contributory scheme there may also be a return of contributions, with or without interest.

The lump sum will normally be payable under discretionary trust to avoid being assessable for inheritance tax and to ensure speedy payment. This means that the recipient is selected at the trustees' discretion from a wide class of possible beneficiaries although they will usually take into account the deceased member's wishes as detailed on the expression of wish form. To give the trustees every chance to make a quick and appropriate decision, members should be encouraged to review their expression of wish forms regularly.

If dependants' pensions are payable, their birth certificates, and where appropriate marriage certificates, will need to be seen (although in most cases these will have been seen at earlier dates – see below). Payment instructions will need to be obtained so that the pensions can commence as soon as possible.

Benefits may also be payable where a member dies in retirement or in service after NPD. For a member in early retirement the scheme may have continued to provide cover for a lump sum death benefit. Spouse's and children's pensions may also be payable. A member's pension may also carry a guarantee on the term of payment, usually five years. Therefore if a pensioner dies within this time after retirement a lump sum representing the unpaid pension instalments is payable (although the pension may instead be paid by simply continuing the instalments until the guarantee period has expired). If a member dies in service having passed the NPD he or she is usually treated as having retired at the date of death.

Finally, a member who has left with entitlement to a deferred pension may die before reaching pension age. In this case there may be a spouse's pension and/or a return of the member's own contributions (with or without interest). Often in this instance the sum involved is small and the trustees may not even know the member has died until some while after the event, but there is little the trustees can do if a former member loses contact. Once the trustees learn of the death they should arrange for the payment of benefits (including any outstanding pension instalments) as soon as possible.

6.3 Record-keeping

From the time an employee joins the company and becomes eligible to join the pension scheme records need to be maintained for him or her. Records are even required in respect of an employee who declines to join in case there are restrictions should he or she subsequently wish to join at a later date. It is vital that the records are comprehensive and that a high level of accuracy is maintained. Apart from the poor impression given to members by inaccurate information, if it results in the wrong person receiving the benefit, the trustees (who are ultimately responsible for the administration of the scheme) will have committed a breach of trust, with all the liabilities which that invokes. Many of these records will duplicate information held by the employer's personnel department and so there may be cost savings to be made by combining the two. However, since the information is being held for two different purposes (pensions and personnel) it may not be practicable for the two sets of records to be combined.

The storage and retrieval of such large amounts of information is of course an ideal subject for computerisation. However, care must be taken to comply with the provisions of the Data Protection Act 1984 (see below). For this reason many smaller schemes run largely by the employer still have manual records.

Now that membership of an occupational pension scheme is voluntary it is important for personnel staff and managers to be in a position to explain details of the company's pension arrangements to new recruits. In many cases the company may operate different arrangements such as a final salary scheme and a group personal pension arrangement. Even if an employee is not eligible to join a scheme immediately he or she should be given information so that, when eligible to join, he or she can make a decision. For this reason, scheme documentation, including explanatory literature, should be kept up to date.

6.3.1 Member records

A new member will be required to complete an application form giving brief personal information such as full name, sex, date of birth and agreeing to member contributions (if applicable) to be deducted from salary or wages. At the same time information may be sought about retained benefits from a previous pension arrangement. Details will also be required if a member currently contributes to an FSAVC arrangement or a personal pension. The application form or a separate expression of wish form (also called a nomination form) will ask the member to indicate the person(s) to whom he or she would like the lump sum death benefit to be paid. The information provided by the member will be supplemented by information from the company such as date of entry to service, NI number, location (if it is a multi-site employer) and pensionable salary details.

This information forms the basic member record which is then built up during the period of scheme membership with historical records of salary together with contributions and NI earnings if applicable. It is advisable from time to time to issue members with their member record card to check the basic information.

6.3.2 Verification

When a member joins the scheme his or her date of birth should be verified against his or her birth certificate and the fact that this has been done should be recorded. Similarly if spouse's benefits are provided, the spouse's date of birth and proof of marriage should be obtained. Employees should be encouraged to keep the pensions department advised of any change in marital status and the number of dependent children and to provide sight of children's birth certificates. Verification obviously includes marriage and the birth of children but also divorce and death. At these times a member should also be asked whether his or her expression of wish form needs updating. Remember that consideration is being given to the splitting of pensions on divorce so further information will need to be held subsequently.

6.3.3 Medical evidence

Where death-in-service benefits are insured the insurance company will operate a 'free cover' level. This is the amount, usually expressed in benefit terms, below which cover is provided automatically without the member being required to provide evidence of the state of his or her health, either by completing a questionnaire, or by undergoing a medical examination. For example the free cover level for a lump sum of 4 × salary may be £160,000. This would mean that anyone with a salary of £40,000 or less is automatically covered. However, members with salaries above this amount may be asked to provide evidence of health. If the evidence obtained is then unsatisfactory the insurer may impose restrictions on the level of cover for that member or alternatively request higher premiums or even decline the risk. Whilst the underwriting for these individuals is being undertaken it is possible they will only be covered for life assurance up to the free cover limit and therefore other temporary insurance will be required. There is therefore a danger that the scheme and trustee can inadvertently be promising death-in-service benefits which are temporarily uninsured. If a claim occurred during this uninsured period the scheme could suffer.

6.3.4 Transfer records

An employee may have retained benefits from a previous employer's scheme, a personal pension or an FSAVC policy. In due course he or she may wish to consider transferring these benefits into the new scheme. The administrators of the new scheme will need to obtain information concerning the previous arrangement including the type of arrangement, details of the benefit and any increases applicable to it, the transfer value being offered and any contracted-out information. If the member decides to proceed with the transfer then this information, together with the benefits secured in the new scheme, will need to be recorded. In addition the period of qualifying service (for preservation purposes), the maximum cash sum and the Inland Revenue rules that applied to the old scheme need to be noted. It can sometimes be more effective to ask the individual to obtain the information from his or her previous employer.

6.3.5 Updating records

In a defined benefit scheme the historical records for each member will normally be updated annually at the scheme renewal date. At this time the employer will be asked for details of salary changes since the last renewal date. In a contributory scheme details of the member contributions must also be supplied and for a contracted-out scheme details of the contracted-out earnings are required.

In a money purchase scheme annual updates for salaries for death-in-service purposes and contracted-out earnings (where applicable) will be adequate. For small insured schemes benefits may be costed individually. The insurance premium accounts would show monthly employer and employee contributions with adjustments in respect of members joining and leaving.

6.3.6 Leavers' records

When a member leaves service it is still necessary for the record to be maintained. If the member receives a refund of contributions or a death benefit is paid resulting in no further liability in the scheme the active record will effectively be closed. Details of the benefit payment will be recorded together with final contribution and contracted-out earnings figures.

If a member leaves with a deferred benefit entitlement, additional information is recorded to show the preserved benefit, the portion subject to revaluation and GMP or protected rights details.

6.3.7 Pension records

When a member retires, or dies leaving a spouse entitled to a pension, the pension may either be bought out with an insurance company or paid from the fund. In the latter case details of individual benefit payments must be recorded. Pay-as-you-earn (PAYE) tax records must be kept for remitting the correct amount to the Inland Revenue and for completing P45/P60 information. This is more often operated through the company payroll with a compensatory payment made from the scheme. For pensions subject to increases, records must be kept so that the increases can be calculated and paid, including details of any GMP element of the pension and the different effective dates on when the increases are to be made.

6.3.8 Scheme financial records

Other than maintaining accurate membership records, adequate financial records must be kept. When a scheme is established the trustees will need to open their own separate bank account. Great care needs to be taken to ensure that this account is kept entirely separate from any of the company's accounts, particularly where they are both held in the same bank branch. It is not unknown for scheme monies to find their way into the company's accounts! The account will allow for receipt of contributions and transfer values as well as payment of pensions, lump sums, refunds and other benefits. The trustees should aim to keep as little money as possible in a non-interest-bearing account.

Procedures need to be set up to record and account for certain payments of tax due to the Inland Revenue, as follows:

1. On contribution refunds, tax deduction at the statutory rate, currently 20 per cent.
2. On pension payments to retired members, widows/widowers of members or other dependants, where income tax is deducted before payment under PAYE.

3. On commutation on grounds of triviality on any amounts in excess of approvable cash limits where again the statutory deduction is at the rate of 20 per cent (except that no tax charge arises where the scheme is or has been contracted-out and a GMP is left preserved in the scheme).
4. On commutation of 100 per cent pension on retirement in exceptional cases of serious ill-health.
5. Tax due on the repayment of additional voluntary contribution excess funds.
6. Tax due on refunds of surplus to the employer.

In addition, in the case of a self-administered scheme investing in anything other than a tax-exempt fund, the scheme may be able to reclaim at least some of the tax paid on the investments. This most commonly arises in respect of Advance Corporation Tax deducted from dividends on UK equities held by the scheme.

The actual payment of the tax to the Inland Revenue arising from 1, 3 and 4 is usually made after the end of the tax year. A return is submitted to the Inspector of Taxes showing the amounts refunded or commuted and the tax deducted. This is offset against any refunds of tax due to the fund, although a large fund may be able to reclaim tax paid on investments more frequently.

6.3.9 Data Protection Act 1984

Where the pension scheme records are held on a computer, care must be taken to ensure that the provisions of this Act are complied with. It is usual for the trustees, administrator and employer to be registered for the purposes of the pension scheme. Even where none of the administration is done in-house it may be necessary for the trustees nevertheless to register for this purpose. Registration should outline the following:

1. Which data are retained.
2. The source of information.
3. The use to which the data are put.
4. To whom the data are given.

Registered parties need also to observe the eight principles of data protection:

1. Data must be obtained fairly.
2. Data must be held only for the specified purpose.
3. Data must not be disclosed, except to the individual or his or her agent or as set out in the Register.
4. Data must be adequate, relevant and not excessive for its registered purpose.
5. Data must be accurate and up to date.

6. Data must not be retained for longer than is necessary.
7. Data must be secure and isolated from unauthorised access, destruction or loss.
8. The individual in respect of whom data are held must be given reasonable access to the data and have a right to have inaccuracies corrected.

There are certain exemptions in respect of pension schemes but you should always check that as trustees you are not holding additional information which is not covered by these exemptions.

6.4 Communication

6.4.1 With the authorities

Pension schemes are closely regulated by the authorities. This can involve a considerable amount of work on behalf of scheme administrators and trustees, not only when establishing the scheme and when making any major changes to it, but also through routine items required as part of the regulatory process. The requirements differ according to the type of scheme involved, and most of them will be handled on the scheme's behalf by any insurer or consultant involved. However, many of the information forms require trustees' or administrators' signatures to certify that correct information has been provided. Of course, the insurer or other adviser involved will need to obtain large amounts of information about the scheme, the members and the company in order to pass this on to the authorities. Furthermore, in the case of a scheme becoming or ceasing to be contracted-out of SERPS, there are official forms and notifications which must be produced by the company itself (although the pensions adviser should help with production of the appropriate wording).

The authorities involved are as follows:

1. The PSO. The Pension Schemes Office is the section of the Inland Revenue charged with regulating pension schemes which qualify for tax relief – whether occupational schemes, PPs, FSAVCs or (formerly) RACs. Its role is to ensure that tax concessions are not abused.
2. The OPB. The Occupational Pensions Board (an executive agency of the DSS) exists primarily to protect the interests of scheme members. As such it is responsible for monitoring and enforcing compliance with the regulations governing preservation, equal access and contracting-out.
3. The Registrar. The Registrar of Occupational Pension Schemes is responsible for running the Register which contains information on all occupational schemes in the United Kingdom.

6.4.2 With members

Effective communication between employers or trustees and the members of the scheme and their dependants is essential if the value of the scheme as an employee benefit is to be fully understood and appreciated. The Disclosure of Information Regulations 1986, as amended, set out requirements as to what needs to be communicated, to whom and within what time limits. Checklist 7 at the end of this chapter gives a summary of these requirements.

There are times when written material needs to be brought to the attention of the membership, such as whenever changes are to be made to the scheme, particularly concerning contracting-out, and this can be done using notices, personal letters or memoranda. The display of notices on a notice board is not usually very effective as they are easily overlooked. It is preferable to use personal letters or memoranda delivered direct to members or included in their pay packets. However this should not be done too frequently otherwise the information will not be given serious attention.

6.4.3 Explanatory booklets and announcements

The first formal communication a member is likely to receive is the scheme booklet which should include full basic details of the scheme and be given within thirteen weeks of membership commencing. Booklets may also be updated by supplementary announcements. Many scheme booklets are unsatisfactory in that they use jargon, are written in an illogical order and are out of date. A booklet is not a substitute for the Trust Deed and Rules but it may be the document upon which the member relies for information about the scheme. As such it must be clear, concise and correct. The writing of such explanatory literature should not be undertaken lightly.

Under the Disclosure of Information Regulations a member is entitled to request a statement of accrued benefits once every twelve months. In practice trustees usually issue benefit statements to all their members annually. These contain details of benefits payable on death and retirement and may also include other scheme information such as the accrued value of AVCs paid and even other employee benefits such as permanent health insurance. In a defined benefit scheme retirement benefits are generally calculated using current remuneration and potential service to NPD. Under a money purchase scheme it is more difficult to give a projection of the likely benefits at retirement. The current fund value based on contributions paid and investment returns to date is usually shown instead.

6.4.4 Trustees' Annual Report

The trustees must also make available an Annual Report which is made up of the trustees' report to members, the investment report showing how the fund has been invested over the year and the returns achieved, full audited accounts and a statement from the actuary about the scheme's solvency.

The trustees' report must include the following:

1. Details of the trustees, how they are appointed and removed, and the trustees' professional advisers.
2. The address to which enquiries about the scheme should be sent.
3. Any recent changes to the basic information on the scheme.
4. The number of members and beneficiaries.
5. Information about increases to pensions in payment.
6. Information about transfer value calculations and payments (i.e. in accordance with actuarial recommendations).
7. Information about contributions (i.e. at a rate recommended by the actuary).
8. A review of the scheme's financial development.
9. Details of the investment manager and basis of remuneration if paid from scheme's assets.
10. A statement confirming whether each trustee has access to a copy of the OPB booklet on trust principles.
11. Details of any self-investment and of steps/proposals to reduce any excessive self-investment.

In addition to the current report, copies of the preceding four reports must be available for inspection.

6.4.5 Other information

In addition to communicating with members as required by legislation, schemes may make use of in-house magazines and staff meetings to impart information. Meetings are often useful if there is a major change taking place such as a company takeover or the introduction of a new scheme. They give members a chance to discuss problems and ask questions face-to-face.

One of the most important points to remember regarding all communication concerning pension matters is the use of plain English. One of the points made in the Goode Report was that scheme members generally neither read nor understand the information which is disclosed to them. This is often due to the fact that documents are not written in plain English and contain liberal helpings of jargon.

Checklist 6   Administration

Registrations and certificates
- Data Protection Act
- Registar of Occupational Pension Schemes
- contracting-out certificate

Day-to-day administration
- information flow between payroll, pensions and personnel
- agreed turn-around times for all entrants and exits
- benefit statements
- contributions due   – member's normal
                             – member's AVCs
                             – company's
  how much and when
- payment of benefits   – checking procedures
                             – delays
                             – cheque signing
- pension increases   – when granted
                             – discretionary
- death benefits   – company policy on payment and advice
- expression of wish forms – up to date
- member's records – let them check
- accounting procedures and investing funds
- tax payment and reclamation
- transfers in   – defined contribution
                             – defined benefit
                             – none
- opting-out and not joining – how many
                                        – reason

Communication
- clarity and ease of understanding
- timeliness and speed of dissemination
- booklets, trustees' reports and regular meetings
  (see Checklist 7 – Disclosure of pension scheme information)

Checklist 7   Disclosure of pension scheme information

General exemptions – unapproved schemes, one-member schemes, death-in-service only schemes, untraceable leavers

Main items to be disclosed	To whom	When
Basic information	• new member • members and prospective members, beneficiaries and recognised trade unions	• within 13 weeks • within 1 month of request and once in any 12 months • any changes must be notified to *all* members within one month following change
Annual Report and accounts	• members and prospective members, beneficiaries and recognised trade unions	• notify within one month of becoming available (current members and trade unions). Must be available within 12 months of the end of the scheme year covered
Individual benefits		
Statements		
• money purchase	• members	• within 12 months of joining and annually
• final salary	• members	• on request, with 2 months of request, once in any 12 months
Death	• adults with rights or options • other members	• within 2 months of notification of death • within 2 months of request, once in any 12 months
Leaving service	• members who have given or received notice • other members	• automically within 2 months of notification • within 2 months of request, once in any 12 months
Transfer value enquiries	• members	• within 2 months of request, once in any 12 months
Scheme wind-up	• members and beneficiaries	• automatically within 1 month of start of wind-up • (full details of benefits) within 3 months of realising assets

There are other items covering insolvency, unpaid employee contributions, transfers in and contribution refunds

Scheme documents	• members and prospective members, beneficiaries and recognised trade unions	• within a reasonable time of request, once in any 12 months
Actuarial valuation	• members and prospective members, beneficiaries and recognised trade unions	• valuation at least once every 3.5 years. Report to be obtained by trustees within 2 years of effective date and made available within 3 months of receipt. Must be provided within a reasonable time following request

Details of items to be disclosed

Basic information	Scheme status	• contracted out, tax approved
	Membership	• eligibility, entry and re-entry, membership conditions, leaving the scheme
	Benefits	• what are they and how calculated, discretionary, guarantees, funded or unfunded, history of pension increases, transfer in and out, normal retirement date
	Contributions	• how calculated, extent of employer's commitment to make up any deficit
	General	• Pensions Ombudsman, Register of Pension Schemes, Occupational Pensions Advisory Service, contact for further information about the scheme
Annual Report and accounts	Accounts	• revenue account, statement of assets and liabilities, purchase and sales of investments, analysis of investments (concentration and self-investment), statement of contributions paid, previous years' figures, any departures from SORP1 (Statement of Recommended Practice 1)
	Report	• audited accounts, actuarial statement (final salary schemes), details of trustees (appointment and removal) and advisers, membership details, acknowledgement that trustees have access to OPB statement on pension trust principles, changes in scheme information, pension increases (discretionary and guaranteed), transfer value statement, investment report (including concentration and self-investment), review of scheme's financial development, unpaid contributions, statement by resigning auditor (where relevant), basis of appointment and remuneration of investment manager, address for enquiries
Statement of individual benefits (always with an address for enquiries)	Benefits statements (salary related)	• for active members a statement of benefits, payable from normal pension age and on subsequent death, based on current pensionable salary with either service to date, or service to normal retirement date. Benefits payable on death in service, date of commencement of pensionable service, the accrual rate or formula for benefits, current pensionable salary and details of any offsets
	Benefits statements (money purchase)	• (in respect of the previous scheme year) the value of protected rights and of other accrued rights (and cash equivalent if different), contributions credited to the member during year split between minimum payments made by employers, DSS incentive payment and balance
	Leaving service	• rights and options on leaving, details of transfer value or refund of contributions and allowance made for discretionary benefits

	Retirement	• details of benefits, payments, changing amounts and rights and options on death
	Death	• rights and options, exercising them
	Transfer benefits	• rights to, and amount of
Scheme documents		• Trust Deed and Rules, amending documents
		• names and addresses of participating employers
		• reference to acts and statutory instruments included in documents
		• areas where documents are overridden
Actuarial valuation and statements	Valuation report (funded final salary schemes)	• clear explanation of funding level and future costs
		• material departures from professional guidance (GN9)
	Statements	• security of accrued rights and percentage security if less than 100% prospective rights
		• method and assumptions

7 Investment matters

Prudent investment of assets lies at the very heart of every successful funded pension scheme. Whether the scheme is of the defined benefit or defined contribution variety (or a combination of both) there will always be at least one party with a personal interest in the investment performance achieved by the scheme's assets. In a defined benefit scheme, for example, successful investment performance can mean the difference between an employer paying a contribution or taking a break for a number of years. The effects of this on the company's financial situation will not remain unnoticed by the finance director! Similarly, in a defined contribution scheme the retirement benefits of the members and their dependants are directly affected by the size of the retirement fund built up for them in the scheme. Given that contributions are usually at a fixed level, clearly successful investment performance of the assets purchased by those contributions can mean the difference between a comfortable retirement and one spent in abject poverty.

However, investment performance is not simply a question of achieving the highest possible returns. With higher potential returns comes greater risk. Also, the sheer number and diversity of possible investment media for today's pension scheme means that a lot of careful thought has to be given to whether the media chosen 'match' the benefits which the scheme is aiming to provide. For example, assets required to provide benefits for a member who is within five years of his or her retirement should not be locked away in an investment medium to which cumulative penalties will apply if it is encashed within ten years. Instead, those assets should be invested in a medium which provides a low risk, relatively stable investment, albeit perhaps with a relatively low return, to avoid the risk of a major failure so close to retirement date that there is not enough time to redress the loss.

Consequently, any investment strategy adopted should be specific to the particular pension scheme and it is the responsibility of the trustees (often working with the company) to identify those objectives and to set an appropriate strategy to achieve them. This is a highly specialised task and requires great skill from the investment manager. Pension scheme trustees rarely have such expertise and are therefore normally expected to delegate this function to a manager. However, trustees remain responsible to the beneficiaries of the scheme for the performance of that manager and so they must take great care when selecting the manager, and also in ensuring that his or her performance meets the required standards and objectives.

The comments in this chapter are written in the context of a self-administered pension scheme, rather than an insured arrangement. However, the same principles apply to all investment management. Where, for example, the scheme is established by means of an insurance company's package, you should still seek to check that the investment strategies and returns are appropriate for your scheme. If you are not satisfied, then consideration should be given to changing the investment medium or manager, either to another insurance company, or by converting the scheme to a self-administered basis and appointing separate outside managers. There will be a number of factors affecting such a decision, and these were dealt with in Chapters 2 and 4.

7.1 Investment powers

It should be remembered that the investment media selected for the scheme's assets may be limited by the scheme's governing documents or by overriding law. The Trustee Investments Act 1961 sets out an investment strategy for all trusts (see Chapter 12 for future proposals). In pension scheme terms its provisions are very restrictive, allowing no more than 50 per cent of the fund to be invested in anything with a higher risk than quoted 'blue chip' equities. The Act is automatically applicable to every trust, unless its provisions are expressly excluded. For this reason, pension schemes commonly have a widely drawn power of investment in their governing documents. The courts, however, will apply any such rule literally and so it is important for trustees to make sure that they understand and follow any restrictions applicable to their particular scheme. When instructing an investment manager, they should also make sure that he or she understands the relevant restrictions. Correspondingly it is essential that the investment powers in the trust deed are kept up to date to reflect current investment trends.

7.2 Investment strategy

Once the benefit basis of the scheme has been decided, it will be up to the trustees (with specialist advice) to map out the investment strategy which they reasonably feel will achieve the aims of the scheme while incurring the minimum risk. This will involve different strategies depending upon the form in which the promised benefits are to be calculated, i.e. whether the scheme is of the defined contribution or defined benefit (or hybrid) variety.

7.2.1 Defined contribution schemes

The investment strategy of a defined contribution scheme can be tailored to the liability profile either of each individual member, or of a group of members. The liability profile is established by looking at the age of the member and the likely date from which he or she will require the scheme to provide benefits. Thus, for example, it may be desirable for investment in respect of younger employees with twenty-five years or more before retirement to be placed in assets offering greater volatility but usually greater long-term reward, such as equities, rather than in less volatile fixed interest securities. However, assets in respect of an employee with only a limited number of years before retirement, say five years or less, would be better placed in media having a lower level of volatility.

7.2.2 Defined benefit schemes

Since a defined benefit scheme promises the individual members a benefit upon retirement, reflecting the number of years each member has been in that scheme and his or her final relevant remuneration, the contribution level is controlled by the defined benefit together with the performance achieved by the scheme assets. Therefore, the investment strategy of such a scheme is usually a reflection of the total of the defined benefit promises (the liabilities) and the required long-term growth of scheme assets to meet those liabilities. Again, you will have to bear in mind the timing and size of calls on the fund as a result of members retiring, leaving or dying, but these considerations are not overly onerous in themselves until the scheme starts to mature and the income coming into the scheme is less than the benefit going out – leading to a sale of assets.

A common overall objective set for these schemes is to achieve an average return above the rate of wage inflation. Historically, this has not been too onerous a task for the average scheme, with the exception of some short periods such as the high-inflationary 1970s. Therefore, in more recent years, investment strategies for such schemes have largely required, and achieved, rather better returns, due largely to their high weightings in and strong performance from equities since the mid-1970s. At the end of 1993 the average final salary pension scheme had the typical asset mix shown in Table 7.1.

Investing the assets in a more conservative manner, however, would be more appropriate if the scheme is mature, or if the trustees wished merely to match wage inflation in terms of performance return. The extent to which pension schemes have been successful in implementing such a strategy in recent years is shown by the fact that the average pension fund return over the ten years to 31 December 1993 was 15 per cent a year whilst the National Average Earnings Index was 7.4 per cent a year and the RPI was 5 per cent a year.

Table 7.1 Average asset distribution of a
final salary pension scheme as at
31 December 1993 (%)

Equities:	UK	58
	overseas	25
Property		2
Fixed interest		12
Cash		3

Extracted from the *Annual Survey of CAPS Ltd.*

For most longer-term periods the investment return on different asset categories suggests that equities out-perform fixed interest stock and property and produce returns in excess of both price and salary inflation as Table 7.2 illustrates. However a warning should be sounded on this

Table 7.2 Annualised returns – periods ending 31 December 1993 (%)

		1 year	5 years	10 years
Equities:	UK	28.4	18.1	18.7
	overseas	24.9	9.5	14.5
Property		14.0	3.2	8.5
Fixed interest		20.8	14.5	12.3
Cash		5.8	11.5	11.1
RPI		1.9	5.2	5.0
Earnings index		3.3	6.8	7.4

Extracted from the *Annual Survey of CAPS Ltd.*

subject as the ten-year returns to December 1981 were very different. These showed an average pension fund return of 11.5 per cent a year against National Average Earnings Index figure of 16 per cent a year and RPI rises of 14.1 per cent a year.

7.3 Investment risk

When implementing an investment strategy, the company, trustees and investment managers must have regard to the risks attached to particular investments. However, 'risk' can take many forms, most of which can be controlled or reduced to acceptable levels.

1. *Market risk* is the danger inherent in any one investment market, such as UK equities. This can be reduced by spreading the portfolio across a number of asset classes to form a balanced asset distribution covering, for example, UK equities, overseas equities, UK fixed interest, international bonds, index-linked securities, direct property and cash.
2. *Sector risk* is the risk attached to any one sector of a market, such as banks or retail stores in UK equities or short-dated stocks among fixed

interest securities. This can be reduced by ensuring that the asset class portfolio is spread across a range of sectors within that class.

3. *Specific risk* is the uncertainty factor in respect of any individual share, where the worst possibility is the total loss of the investment. The impact of such a risk can be significantly reduced by the inclusion of more than twenty-five separate equity holdings.

4. *Benchmark risk* is the possibility of underperforming any specified asset distribution benchmark. This can be reduced by following a similar shape and weighting of assets within any asset class or portfolio type.

5. *Manager risk* is the risk of a particular investment manager failing to deliver the required fund performance, by misreading the markets and wrongly timing purchases and sales, selecting the wrong asset mix, or simply displaying poor stock-picking abilities. This risk can be reduced by appointing more than one manager. In the context of a managed fund or insurance-based investment this can be achieved simply by investing in a mixed fund, where the assets held are in units of a variety of specialist funds, each of which is itself managed by a different manager.

The different parties involved in the pension scheme will have a different interpretation of risk. To the members it can be the loss of fund monies and no pension at retirement or the loss of surplus thereby reducing the opportunity for benefit improvements. To the trustees it can be the insufficiency of assets to provide the benefits promised as they fall due. To the finance director it can be the risk of a volatile or increasing contribution rate.

The search for returns inevitably involves an element of risk. However, unnecessary risk should be avoided. The greatest risk for a pension scheme is the risk that the assets will not grow sufficiently to provide for the promised or hoped-for benefits. This risk can be reduced by reviewing the liability profile and matching the assets with the scheme liabilities.

7.4 Liability profile of the scheme

The liability profile of the scheme is effectively an assessment of the type and value of the benefits which it is required to provide, and the dates from which those benefits are to be paid. Once this has been identified, an appropriate asset profile can be determined. This is achieved by an analysis of the asset/liability profile, or at least a guide as to the best investments to cover those liabilities. This will dovetail with the latest actuarial valuation on the size of the fund likely to be needed to meet the scheme's liabilities and the extent to which the present fund needs to be altered to ensure a close match. (Further details of the actuary's role in fixing the size of the required fund are contained in Chapter 9.)

Any such analysis would be affected by the following:

1. Type of members – active, deferred or pensioner.
2. Active profiles – age, salary and benefit structures.
3. Cash-flow requirement – lump sums, annuity purchases, pensions in payment or transfer value payments.

7.5 Investment vehicle

The two most common investment vehicles for corporate pension schemes are pooled/commingled investments or segregated portfolios (excluding insured schemes which have been considered in Chapter 2).

1. *Pooled funds.* The 'pooled' fund approach uses a single commingled tax-exempt fund, which issues units to a range of pension scheme investors in this fund via the purchase of such units. Pooled funds now exist across specific asset classes but are usually managed/balanced funds with a general performance objective of outperforming the average fund.

   Pooled funds allow small pension schemes to commingle their assets with other similar schemes to form a large pool of assets and thereby benefit from the generally superior returns available to the larger investor and avoid the impact of short-term cash-flow problems on investment decisions.
2. *Segregated funds.* For larger pension schemes, a more appropriate investment vehicle may be a segregated pension portfolio, which invests directly in individual securities, at least in the UK portion and possibly in other areas, if the size of scheme allows. Portfolios managed on a segregated basis clearly offer much greater opportunity for tailor-making stock decisions to that scheme's objectives and will normally be cheaper than pooled arrangements, above a size of some £15–£20m.

Once you have decided on an appropriate manager structure, which may well interact with the decision on the types of vehicle the manager wishes to use and the total size of the assets under management, you will move on to the next key stage in the investment process, that of the appointment of an appropriate investment manager for the role envisaged.

7.6 Investment manager structure

The selection of a particular manager structure for a pension scheme is largely driven by the investment strategy to be followed. If, for example, a specific objective is to be achieved through investments with a high fixed interest content, it may be desirable to appoint a specialist bond manager. However, if the objectives were recognised as being very similar to the average pension fund and managers following appropriate investment policies can be identified, then a single balanced manager may be considered sufficient.

Traditionally in the United Kingdom, pension schemes have had a single 'balanced' fund manager. This describes the use of one investment manager's balanced portfolio or mixed fund. This is simple, cheap and often the best solution for the average medium-sized UK pension scheme. However, as pension schemes mature and become increasingly aware of their liability profiles or members' specific requirements, this traditional structure has become less relevant. The potential variations of manager structure are numerous but the most common are the following:

1. *Dual manager structure.* By splitting the assets between two or more managers, the specific investment manager risk is reduced, especially if the managers have differing investment philosophies and approaches. This also introduces an element of competition to the incumbent managers for the scheme contributions.
2. *Core/satellite structure.* Here again, more than one investment manager is used with the core of the assets sitting in a traditional balanced or indexed fund but a minority proportion, 'the satellite', is invested in either a pure equity fund or overseas fund, or with a strong equity bias for a slightly more aggressive position, or a fund with a fixed interest bias for a slightly more defensive position. The split between core and satellite can range from 60 to 90 per cent in the core, but often tends to be 70 per cent core and 30 per cent satellite.
3. *Multi-specialist structure.* For larger schemes, a structure may be adopted that allows the trustees to appoint specific investment managers to manage particular asset classes, that is, a UK equity investment manager, an overseas equity investment manager, a fixed interest investment manager and so on. Obviously, this is usually restricted to larger schemes (probably with assets in excess of £100m) but allows the trustees to appoint managers in fields of specific expertise. In such circumstances it is important that the trustees work closely with the company and advisers to determine the required asset allocation between the various specialist managers.
4. *Other structures.* There are many other possible structures involving the use of indexed funds which try to match a particular market index such as the FT 100 share index. Larger funds can sometimes appoint specialist managers to review and take advantage of shorter-term market movements (known as tactical asset allocation) or incorporate options and futures as well as currency hedges into the strategy to avoid the impact of volatile stock price movements (sometimes known as portfolio insurance). However, the scope of this book does not embrace a review of the more esoteric aspects of pension scheme investments.

There is no clear definition of an ideal manager structure for a particular strategy but often the liability profile, amount of assets under management, surplus position and the sophistication of the investors will control the decision.

Manager selection

The impact that a good investment manager can have on a pension scheme's ability to pay its liabilities, or on the contribution rate that a sponsor ultimately has to meet, should not be underestimated. An apparently minor improvement in investment performance can result in a significant reduction in contribution requirement from the sponsor and/or enable improvements in scheme benefits. The effect is, perhaps, even more apparent in defined contribution schemes with the ultimate benefit being heavily dependent on the investment return.

An indication of the likely benefits that can be gained from a good investment manager can be gauged by an examination of pension fund returns. Over the five years ending 31 December 1993, the upper quartile manager outperformed the lower quartile manager by approximately 12.5 per cent. For a pension fund of £1m this would produce an additional £125,000 which could be used to increase benefits or reduce contributions. This certainly will focus the minds of both the trustees and the scheme's sponsors and will encourage them to invest both time and effort in making sure the initial framework, in terms of the objective and strategy, is in place and that the most appropriate fund manager for that strategy is appointed.

Unfortunately, in the past, the appointment of investment managers has been achieved through many routes and, more often than not, it has been driven more by recent performance than an in-depth analysis of the potential to achieve good results in the future. It is true that past performance is probably the only readily recognisable piece of objective analysis that is widely available to trustees. Most do not have the time, nor usually the expertise, to assess the capabilities of the many and varied investment managers offering management services to pension funds – but their advisers can help.

The selection of an investment manager for a pension scheme will always carry an element of chance. Therefore, the objective of any manager selection process must be to reduce that element to an acceptable level. If the process is conducted in a disciplined manner, you should feel comfortable with the selection, in the knowledge that the investment manager has a clear understanding of the fund's objectives and the strategy being adopted in order to achieve them.

The main areas on which the trustees should focus when selecting an investment manager are as follows:

1. Investment philosophy.
2. Investment process.
3. Investment personnel.
4. Manager's plan and business mix.
5. Investment administration.
6. Communication with trustees and advisers.
7. Custodianship.

Although many investment managers claim to have similar philosophies and objectives, differences will be found in various areas. It is usual that the deeper the analysis of a manager becomes, the more apparent these differences are.

It is essential that the investment manager clearly understands your specified strategy and profile and is able to describe how he or she intends to fulfil such a mandate on the trustees' behalf.

7.8 Monitoring of manager performance

As mentioned earlier it is vital that, when setting the investment objectives and deciding on the strategy to achieve these objectives, you have specific goals in mind and recognise the need to set the investment manager specific benchmarks for the achievement of these goals. The pension fund will usually have a total fund benchmark and also a benchmark for each of the separate asset classes in which it invests. For example, in respect of UK equities, it might have a benchmark of a specified outperformance of the FT All Share Index, whilst still having a total fund objective of a survey upper quartile over rolling five-year periods.

If the investment manager is consistently underperforming these benchmarks, a number of actions can be taken. Firstly, if underperformance is in one specific asset category and the portfolio is of sufficient size, it may be appropriate to move from an active investment management style to a passive or indexed manager style for that asset class. This may result in the movement of assets from that particular investment manager, or it may involve switching the assets from an actively managed fund into a passively managed fund within the same investment house's portfolio of funds. If, however, the underperformance is more significant and widespread and you become disenchanted with the investment manager's abilities, it is more likely to result in dismissal. The cost of transferring assets from one investment manager to another can vary significantly, depending on the nature of the investments being altered. There is little doubt that in extreme cases, such as a switch from an insurance policy to a directly invested portfolio, this can be expensive. In other cases, however, the costs can be more reasonable.

The cost of transferring assets from one pooled fund investment manager to another is usually between 1 and 2 per cent of the total value of the assets. Transferring a segregated portfolio could cost from close to 0 to around 2 per cent, depending on the initial switching in the portfolio's securities immediately following transfer. In terms of the potential improvement in performance that can accrue when moving from a poorly performing investment manager to a successful one, this cost can clearly be relatively insignificant.

Checklist 8   Investment matters

Investment restrictions in scheme rules

Liability profile	– cash flows
	– security

Attitude to risk	– sectors
	– stocks

Performance	– benchmark
	– targets
	– period of measurement

Quality and frequency of investment manager's reporting

Investment structure	– one or several managers
	– pooled or segregated funds
	– core and satellites
	– balanced
	– indexed funds

8 Security and protection of members' interests

Following the Maxwell affair the issue of the security of scheme assets has been thrown sharply into focus. It is certainly true that there was a good deal of complacency prior to this highly publicised failure. Much has been done to tighten up security, but it should be noted that no organisation can guarantee security absolutely, nor is any organisation prepared to say that the assets are absolutely secure. However sophisticated the procedures are, no one can fully protect against the determined crook. However, by responding to the issues raised and revising current practices, if necessary, the risk can be reduced to an acceptable level.

This is a very real issue for the trustees. In many cases they will not hold assets themselves, nor even necessarily the pieces of paper proving title. Nevertheless, even where they have delegated investment management to outside bodies, and custody of scheme assets has also been transferred, they remain ultimately responsible for ensuring the security of those assets. They therefore have a strong personal interest in the matter as trustees, whether or not they are also members!

Most pension scheme trust deeds purport to give some indemnity to protect the trustees. However, such an indemnity goes against the established principles of trust law, and has yet to be properly tested in the courts. In any case, conscientious trustees should not be seeking to rely on indemnities: they should arrange matters so that the risk of an asset loss is reduced to a minimal level. In this chapter we set out the main security issues and suggest ways of minimising risk.

8.1 Insurance policies and pooled funds

Many schemes (particularly the smaller ones) invest in insurance policies which are tied in to give an exact match of the trustees' liabilities to members (whether through a series of individual policies earmarked for the benefit of particular members, or through a single pooled fund covering the scheme's liabilities). Still more invest in managed funds (pooled funds) held by insurance companies or other professional fund managers. In these cases, trustees will get a statement of their units in the fund and this constitutes their document evidencing good title to the assets. No other documents are required in this respect.

Insurance policies are the contracts evidencing the payment of monies into the insurance company concerned and the benefits to be paid out in return. The monies covered by the policy are also invested by the insurance company in a pooled fund which also contains the investments represented by policies of other policyholders with that insurer. As with managed funds, the policyholder does not have title to the actual assets held by the fund, and so never gets to see the actual investments themselves. There is little therefore that a policyholder or managed fund investor can do to check the security of the assets underlining the share of the pooled fund. The security of these funds is covered by their being regulated by the appropriate statutory regulatory organisation (SRO such as SIB, IMRO, PIA) and the Treasury and those bodies monitor the procedures of the fund managers to ensure that security is adequately protected. In the unlikely event that a fund managed by a reputable manager fails because of a breach in security, the policyholders would be compensated, in the event of total failure, to the extent of 90 per cent of their holdings under the Policyholders Protection Act; if the failure was only partial, one would expect the loss to the fund to be made up by indemnity insurance carried by the fund manager, and failing that the loss would be apportioned over all the units involved.

Consequently in respect of insured or managed fund arrangements, the trustees will have very little control over security aspects once the money is within the appropriate fund. Where they will be directly concerned, however, is where the money is going into or coming out of the appropriate policy or managed fund. For such situations the trustees should institute their own procedures to ensure that monies can only be paid out of the policy to a secure account under the trustees' control. This is an aspect of asset movement control which is dealt with separately later in this chapter.

8.2 Self-administered schemes

Most of the larger schemes will have dedicated portfolios of assets, usually managed by external fund managers. Included in these portfolios may well be some insurance or managed fund policies as described above, but the majority of assets will be direct holdings in shares, stocks, gilts, cash, real property, futures and sometimes even 'pride of possession' investments such as works of art, vintage motor cars and vintage wines held in bonded warehouses.

Where such investments are directly held by the trustees in their names, then clearly they must think closely about the security of the assets. In the case of land for example, all the trustees should be named as owners (except where the law will not permit it, e.g. where there are more than four trustees) and other documents giving proof of ownership should be locked in a safe or entrusted to the custody of a reputable independent custodian, who should be given specific instructions as to the circumstances under which custody of the asset or its evidence of title can be released.

Most often, however, schemes which have directly invested portfolios will give the management of that portfolio to a professional fund manager, such as a stockbroker. Indeed, very few trustees will directly invest by themselves, because to do that they would need to be registered with an SRO under the Financial Services Act 1986. Consequently, they normally appoint a manager subject to a discretionary management agreement whereby the trustees set out the guidelines for the manager to follow, and leave the day-to-day investment decisions to the manager. The trustees will review performance periodically. In such situations, the fund manager usually holds documents of title such as share certificates. This enables him or her to act swiftly in changing investments. Investments are usually therefore held in the name of the manager's nominee company and frequently that company will be responsible also for the custody of the documents of title. The management of the fund will be subject to a manager's agreement. This should be in one of the standard forms agreed by the manager's appropriate regulatory authority. It will give details of the custody arrangements and will ask for the trustees' agreement to the assets being held in the name of its nominee company. Failure of the manager's procedures which results in a loss to the investor should be compensated through the appropriate regulatory organisation's compensation fund.

For particularly large schemes (over £100m) trustees are increasingly appointing external custodians, that is a custodian independent of the investment manager. This splitting of roles is often opposed by investment managers, partly because of the loss of income through additional fees involved through performing the function themselves, but also because of the loss of control and therefore reduction in the speed of execution. It also makes the arrangements more complicated.

There are similar problems as regards security with both approaches, however. The manager may well limit liability in that he or she will not accept responsibility for the failure of a third party, be it an agent of the manager, or an external custodian. Trustees should therefore take steps to ensure that the custodian or agent concerned has effected suitable insurance to cover losses through, for example, misappropriation and they should also require evidence each year that such insurance remains in force, covering an appropriate amount.

As with the insured and managed fund arrangements described above, trustees will need to ensure that they give clear instructions to fund managers and custodians if appropriate as to how, and upon whose authority, assets may be transferred out of the manager's or custodian's control.

8.2.1 Stock lending

This is a specialist activity which is unlikely to be used by any but the largest schemes. It entitles the owner of a particular security or portfolio to lend it to a money broker, who will provide collateral to the lender for the borrowing of that security or portfolio. The money broker in turn will lend that security to a 'market maker' who requires that particular security/portfolio for a period. Genuine stock-lending arrangements can provide useful additional income to larger funds, but trustees must take great care to ensure that proper safeguards are in place to protect the stock concerned. The process acquired a bad name in the Maxwell scandal when stock was supposedly 'lent', but in fact the arrangements were not proper lending because the pension scheme's interest in the lent stock was not recorded when it was passed on to a third party. Consequently when the Maxwell empire ran into severe financial difficulties, a number of different parties were left claiming title over the same assets. If the trustees wish to indulge in stock lending, either by themselves or under the control of the outside professional manager, they should ensure that sufficient safeguards are in place so that the trustees' interest in the appropriate stock will always be brought to the notice of any third party.

8.2.2 'Security loop'

The need for trustees to institute procedures for the movement of monies to and from investment managers is but one part of a wider issue of how trustees can ensure that assets under their direct control are always secure. There are various ways of doing this, depending upon the particular asset concerned:

1. *Cash.* Here simple precautions will suffice. Cheques drawn on scheme bank accounts should always be signed by at least two signatories. Larger amounts may require the signature of three people. These may not necessarily be the trustees themselves, but clearly any other nominated signatories should be carefully vetted before being authorised.

2. *Movement of money from and between outside managers.* Managers' agreements should include in them (or have annexed to them) specific instructions as to the number and identity of signatures required to disinvest the scheme's assets. The procedures will probably be similar to those covering the validity of cheques on bank accounts. In addition, where the trustees wish to change investment managers, or implement some other strategic investment change, this should require the signature of at least two of the trustees, with the requirement that (where the amount involved exceeds a certain minimum) those trustees should

notify all the other trustees within twenty-four hours after such an instruction has been given.

In this way a 'loop' can be created whereby assets can be moved around under the control of the trustees, but where they cannot break out of the trustees' control without the agreement of the majority.

8.2.3 The role of the auditor

Pension schemes are required to produce audited accounts annually. In the process of undertaking such an audit, the auditor should 'through the normal professional channels' obtain independent verification of the stocks held on behalf of the scheme. These stocks and other assets purchased for the scheme are registered in the name of the investment manager's nominees. However, UK equities share certificates may be marked with client designations, depending on the particular custodian's practices.

In the past, auditors have not always performed this task particularly effectively. However, there is growing evidence to suggest that, particularly following the Maxwell affair, they are taking this part of their role more seriously. Trustees should question their auditors to ensure that they have conducted a thorough investigation into this aspect and are properly satisfied with the results.

For the future, the 1995 Pensions Act requires that auditors should have a new 'whistle-blowing' function and should be required to report to the new Pensions Regulator any circumstances discovered in the process of the audit which are in their opinion in any way suspicious. There will be penalties on auditors for failing to comply with this requirement. Consequently trustees should expect auditors in the future to take more interest in such matters.

8.2.4 Self-investment

Self-investment occurs when assets of the pension scheme are invested back in the sponsoring company. This is usually in the form of a loan-back of monies to the employer or the purchase of some of the employer's shares. It can, however, also take more subtle routes such as the purchase of property or capital assets which are then leased back to the employer. The purchase of assets or land for lease-back can also be undertaken in partnership with the employing company.

In essence, there is no reason why self-investment should not take place. Since occupational pension schemes in the United Kingdom are funded, employers are committed to placing often substantial amounts of money into the hands of trustees for the future benefit of employees. That money is then effectively out of the reach of the company and is therefore unavailable for use in the business. The trustees, on the other hand, having received this money, are obliged to invest it to produce a reasonable return. There is a strong argument for saying that the two interests can be combined and that the trustees can invest in the employing company so that both interests are served.

However, there are many practical reasons why this principle needs to be implemented only with extreme care in practice:

1. One of the advantages of funding pension schemes is that the pension promise for the members is, in theory at least, always covered by assets held by the trustees. A pension at retirement is therefore the only part of an employee's income from his employment which is not directly (to the extent that it has already been funded) dependent upon the performance of the company. If the company goes into liquidation, therefore, and the employees lose their jobs, at least they will have their pension earned up to that date fully protected. However, if any part of the assets guaranteeing that pension are also invested in the company, then the future pension is also jeopardised, along with future employment prospects. This is especially so since pension scheme trustees stand in line with ordinary creditors on a company's insolvency.

2. Because of the close relationship between the sponsoring employer and the scheme (especially where company managers are also the trustees, but also where trustees generally are employees and subject to management pressure in the ordinary course of their work) there may be a great temptation to invest scheme monies back in the employer on terms which are somewhat less than purely commercial. Trustees should never agree to such an action, since it is clearly a breach of trust. However, many such transactions have possibly occurred in the past and have either gone unchallenged or the extent of the 'non-commerciality' of the transaction has not been sufficient to justify the cost of an action against the trustees. Where the scheme provides benefits on a defined contribution basis, it is the members who lose directly from such a transaction. In the case of defined benefit schemes where the employer pays the balance of cost, the loss is arguably less important, since the resulting poor investment performance should work its way through to higher contribution rates later on. However, the important aspect here is that there is a deferment of the eventual cost to the employer – which of course is very often the reason why such a transaction is so attractive to the employer in the first place. If, before proper amends can be made, the employer goes into liquidation, then there is a direct loss to the scheme which will directly affect the benefits of the members.

3. The purchase of land or other assets to be used by the employer may also cause problems for the scheme. Although the trustees do have an asset which they can in theory sell or lease again in the event of the

employer's insolvency, very often such assets are specialised and of use effectively only to the former employing company. The asset may therefore be rendered worthless by the insolvency of the employing company.

Self-investment can therefore be a particular problem for pension schemes, since as noted above there are no special protections available under general law to help trustees recover such losses in the event of company insolvencies. (Contrast this with the situation, which is often also classed as self-investment, where the company fails to pay contributions to the scheme at the agreed rate and frequency. This is strictly self-investment because the money technically belongs to the trustees, but is being retained by the company for its own use. In such a situation, following the insolvency of the employer, the trustees have a first call within limits on the remaining assets of the company (if any) under the deficiency regulations.)

For all these reasons there are now statutory restrictions on self-investment. Their effect is to prohibit self-investment to a greater extent than 5 per cent of the scheme's assets. Self-investment for this purpose includes direct investment by way of loan-back, purchase of shares or failure to pass on due contributions, but also includes purchase of property which is then leased back to the company for its business use. Strangely enough (in common with many of the regulations currently governing occupational pension schemes), there is no penalty on trustees who self-invest in contravention of these regulations apart from cancellation of the contracted-out certificate where relevant. However, trustees do have to disclose in their Annual Report to members any self-investment in excess of the 5 per cent limit, and comment on what they intend doing about reducing it. Unfortunately, once again, there is currently no direct penalty for failure to disclose properly in the Annual Report, so some cases of self-investment may go unnoticed. The regulations also do not currently cover the purchase and loan-back of other assets which may only be of use to the employing company.

A number of schemes have now moved to a position where they permit no self-investment whatsoever, for the reasons already noted. This is certainly a desirable aim, but care has to be taken that self-investment does not occur inadvertently through the investment being in a managed fund which happens, from time to time, to hold shares in the employing company. However, in such a situation the pooled nature of the fund would reduce the loss to the fund in the event of the company's insolvency and so may well be considered to be a risk of ordinary proportions which is normally borne by investors. Also, accidental self-investment of this nature would be unlikely to exceed the statutory 5 per cent limit.

Trustees should therefore consider very carefully whether they wish to become involved in self-investment. Remember, it is their decision (subject to the 5 per cent limit), and they should not allow themselves to be influenced in any way by the company's situation. Having said that, however, trustees are frequently approached by sponsoring employers to self-invest to cover a short-term financial crisis. They then have to balance their members' interests in using some of the fund to keep the company afloat and the members in employment, against the use of an investment which, under the circumstances, must be classified as 'high risk'. Such a decision is one for the trustees to take in any particular case, but the emphasis must surely be on covering the current liabilities, rather than speculating with the assets in the hope of protecting other interests which are outside the fund and therefore outside the direct responsibility of the trustees. Investment back in the employer company under these circumstances could well lead to an action against the trustees for breach of trust in the event of subsequent insolvency of the company and scheme.

There is one exemption from the need to comply with the self-investment regulations. This is in respect of small self-administered schemes. Such schemes are commonly set up for directors and major shareholders of smaller companies. In deference to the need to keep their entrepreneurial spirit alive, they are specifically allowed to self-invest up to 50 per cent of the scheme's assets (25 per cent in the first two years of the scheme's life) provided that the basis of the investment is on purely commercial terms, all the members are trustees and that they all specifically agree to the self-investment. For the purposes only of these regulations, the definition of self-investment does not include the purchase of property which is then leased back for use by the company – as far as the regulations are concerned, therefore, the whole of the fund could be used in such a way.

8.3 Remedies available to beneficiaries

So far we have looked at the question of security from the point of view of the fund and the trustees. However, beneficiaries have their own individual interests under the scheme which are the subject of several different forms of protection.

8.3.1 Occupational Pensions Advisory Service

This organisation, known as OPAS, is a nationwide network of volunteer advisers who are experienced pensions professionals acting independently in accordance with the OPAS Code of Practice. They are backed up by a central panel of experts who specialise in defined areas of pensions work. OPAS is funded by a grant from the DSS, but is entirely independent of all organisations, including the DSS. The service is available to individuals who believe that they have pension rights which, for whatever reason, are not being fulfilled. The organisation operates by negotiation and conciliation and relies on the goodwill of scheme authorities. OPAS cannot deal with complaints by groups, and does not provide a conciliation or arbitration service.

8.3.2 Pensions Ombudsman

The Ombudsman was appointed under the Social Security Act 1990 to deal with complaints against, and disputes with, occupational and personal pension schemes. He or she is completely independent and acts as an impartial adjudicator. As with OPAS, the service offered is not charged to the user. In general, the Ombudsman can investigate complaints of injustice caused by maladministration by the trustees or managers of a scheme, and disputes of fact or law with the trustees or managers. However, the Ombudsman cannot investigate complaints which are the subject of court proceedings, whether past or present. As with OPAS, the Ombudsman can only deal with complaints from individuals. He or she shares an office with OPAS, and frequently has cases referred from that body when it is unable to make progress. (For proposed changes see Chapter 12.)

8.3.3 Court action

Ever since trust law has been in existence, there have been remedies through the court system against trustees and others for breach of trust. This is a wide-ranging area and involves the possibility of many different heads of claim. However, as with all litigation today, this is potentially a very expensive exercise and should only be contemplated by scheme beneficiaries as a last resort. One advantage which such a remedy may have over OPAS or the Ombudsman, however, is that 'representative' actions may be heard, and groups of beneficiaries may pursue a claim. Furthermore, the full range of legal remedies is available, with the full force of the law behind them.

The problem over potential costs can be circumvented by the use of what is known as a 'Beddoes' application. This is an application prior to proceeding with the full hearing of the complaint, and which determines in advance the way in which the costs of the action are to be apportioned. The intention of pursuing such an action is to obtain a court order so that the applicant's costs will be met out of the pension scheme's assets, thereby in practice removing any practical restraint upon the pursuance by a beneficiary or group of beneficiaries of a valid action against the trustees. In this situation the trustees themselves will either have been given the right to defend themselves, charging the cost out to the fund, or they will be indemnified by the company or possibly through separate insurance. The use of these orders is becoming more widespread and will probably lead to a steady growth in litigation involving pension schemes and their members.

8.3.4 Pensions Regulator

The Regulator does not yet exist: the appointment is recommended by the Goode Committee and the Government's White Paper and incorporated in the 1995 Pensions Act. It is envisaged that his or her contribution to scheme security would take the form of involvement in the following ways:

1. To monitor schemes and enforce compliance with legal requirements, including rules related to trustees, minimum solvency and disclosure.
2. To intervene in scheme administration where the scheme assets appear to the Regulator to be in jeopardy.
3. To receive and investigate complaints of impropriety in the management of pension schemes or the composition or conduct of trustees.
4. To disqualify from acting in the management of an occupational pension scheme those who have shown themselves unfit so to act.
5. In defined circumstances, to monitor schemes that are being wound-up or require them to be wound-up.
6. To disseminate information and advice to the public about pension schemes.
7. To issue or approve standards and codes of practice.

If the office of Regulator is created it will probably be funded by the pensions industry but will nevertheless provide a low cost alternative to litigation for disgruntled scheme beneficiaries.

9 Paying for the benefits

Regardless of the way the pension benefits are structured – defined contribution or defined benefit – the company will normally be making a regular contribution. Under the defined contribution approach the contribution is fixed and the final benefits unknown. However, there is a need from the outset and subsequently to estimate the benefits likely to emerge at retirement.

The benefits under a defined benefit scheme are also unknown. Although the formula for calculating the benefits is set, it is normally based on earnings near to retirement which are not known and have to be estimated to determine the regular payment required to build up a fund of assets sufficient to provide the pension at retirement.

In either case the assessment of future benefits and contribution rates is the realm of the actuary.

9.1 The actuary's role

Every defined benefit pension scheme must, by law, receive actuarial advice. The actuary is required to provide the valuations and certificates set down in legislation. Nevertheless, the actuary can and should be doing much more to help the employer generally with all pensions matters. Guiding the employer on the pensions cost, keeping it even (if that is what the employer requires), avoiding unexpected surprises and producing imaginative solutions when special packages are required are his or her prime responsibilities. The actuary's knowledge of investment and investment performance can help the scheme in the choice of investment managers and in the performance of the investments. If pension increases are discretionary, the actuary can give guidance on the amount of increase that can be afforded and whether this can match inflation or whatever other target has been set.

The actual cost of a defined benefit pension scheme can never be known in advance. In fact it is a truism to say that the cost can never be known until the last beneficiary has died. Because the benefits are defined and not the cost, the employer bears the risk and is the guarantor of the scheme but with the ultimate exit route of winding-up if the cost becomes unacceptable (although subject always to the proviso that benefits accrued to date must be fully covered). The actuary guides the employer and trustees on what should be set aside and whether there is enough in the kitty for the security of the accrued rights for members. This is in no way an exact science and despite the complexity of the calculations the end result is only as good as the assumptions made. All the actuary can say is what he or she thinks a prudent person should contribute against the liabilities.

This can be approached in two ways. One can be a reasonably cautious and secure basis providing the margin of safety that scheme members (and trustees) might like to see in place. The alternative is to use what has become known as a 'best estimate' basis which, from the limits of possibility to forecast, is meant to be realistic with roughly equal chances of being too low as too high.

The finances of a pension scheme will be affected by general economic circumstances and by those relating to the particular employment and the scheme. On a broad basis there will be the level of inflation, levels of interest rates and investment performance generally. For example the 1980s, when profits and dividends were rising strongly, resulted in healthy surpluses in many schemes. The position of a particular scheme will be influenced by the salary progression of employees, the incidence of retirements, the age distribution, the actual performance of investment management and many other factors particular to the individual situation. It would be over-optimistic to suggest that the actuary will take account of all these in advance but at least he or she can guide on the key influences and possible effects of variations in them. The actuary will also help by advising on transfer values, costs of improvements either for individuals or to the scheme generally, early retirements, special recruitment packages and so on.

In his or her statutory role the actuary has to provide certificates of solvency (two if the scheme is contracted-out). The first is the one which goes with the trustees' Annual Report and gives the members the assurance that both the assets already in the scheme and the ongoing contribution rate are adequate for their protection. The second certificate for contracted-out schemes is to confirm to the OPB that the GMPs are and will be secure. However, the actuary also has to give a certificate to the Inland Revenue to say that there is not too much money in the scheme since otherwise the Inland Revenue could be losing tax revenues because of the tax shelter given to money held within an approved pension fund.

One further contribution that the actuary has to make is in dealing with the statements required in company accounts according to the accounting standard SSAP24. This should normally be on the best estimate basis mentioned above.

From all of this it is clear that there needs to be a regular dialogue between the actuary, the trustees, the company and the other parties responsible for running the scheme. The actuary cannot perform the job properly unless he or she is aware of the current and future needs at any time of the other parties.

9.2 Defined contribution schemes

It is commonly held that one advantage of a defined contribution scheme is that one does not need an actuary! Since the contribution rates are fixed, the benefits simply emerge accordingly and that should be the end of professional involvement. In practice the actuary can certainly help in setting the contributions in the first place if any attempt is to be made to set targets for the emerging pensions. He or she can also explain how the individual members' accounts are progressing compared with the targets and indicate a reasonable range of possible pensions likely to emerge in practice, both at normal and early retirement.

Defined contribution schemes will also need monitoring to see how the investments are performing and whether the chosen investment house or insurance company seems a reasonable one to retain. Small self-administered schemes, even when providing only defined contribution benefits must be valued every three years by an actuary.

However, for the remainder of this chapter we shall concentrate on the financing of defined benefit plans, where there is normally a range of acceptable solutions which the actuary can propose and it is for the company and trustees – as well as the actuary – to balance the interests of security and company contributions.

9.3 The actuarial valuation

The actuarial valuation is the foundation of the financing of defined benefit schemes. The process is essentially simple although it involves complex mathematics. Using a set of assumptions (see below) the actuary estimates the likely future benefit payments from and investment returns to the pension scheme in respect of the current membership. By discounting these back to the present date a 'present value' of the future benefits and future investment returns is obtained.

Normally this exercise is done in two stages:

1. The first, looking at the benefits and assets which have accrued to date.
2. The second, looking at future benefit accruals and contributions.

In the first, looking at the benefits and assets which have accrued to date, if there are excess assets, there is a surplus. Where the liabilities exceed the assets there is a deficit. The ratio of assets to liabilities for an ongoing scheme is commonly known as the funding level.

At the second stage the actuary is attempting to identify the future contribution rate required to provide for the benefits which will accrue in the future. This contribution rate will be adjusted to take account of any surplus or deficit then existing in the scheme. The calculations should be done assuming the scheme is on-going and then separately as if it were to be terminated. The latter set of figures helps to assess the short-term risk to the security of members' benefits.

9.3.1 Funding method

There are many actuarial methods used to determine the company's future contribution rate. These funding methods as they are known have different uses. Some are more appropriate for schemes which have an ongoing membership and are closed to new entrants. Others need to make allowance for new entrants as they assume the membership profile remains unchanged. It is important therefore that the actuary discusses the method he or she proposes with the company and trustees and establishes whether or not there are any proposals which could affect the suitability of the method.

9.3.2 Assumptions

All actuarial calculations have, by their very nature, to make assumptions about the future. It is the combined effect of all the assumptions together with the funding method that determines whether the actuarial valuation is based on a reasonable model of the future. No single assumption should be considered in isolation.

There is a range of acceptable sets of assumptions which lead to 'cautious' and 'optimistic' funding levels and contribution rates. The actuary's role is to ensure the company and trustees are aware of this range and the consequences of pursuing one set rather than the other. However, in view of the long-term nature of the calculations (it can be over sixty years before an individual who has just joined the pension scheme draws his or her last pension instalment, and longer where there is a younger dependant), it is desirable to be prudent in making these assumptions.

There are essentially two sets of assumptions: demographic and financial. The demographic assumptions cover such areas as the following:

1. Mortality of current active members and their dependants.
2. Mortality of pensioners and their dependants.
3. Marital status – age and sex-related.
4. Proportion leaving service based on age, sex and service.
5. Rate of ill-health and early retirement based on age, sex and service.
6. New entrants' rates by age and sex.

Rarely are schemes large enough to justify an analysis of the scheme experience in these areas and the actuary will tend to use standard tables and take account of any recent scheme experience which may influence these assumptions. However, it is important that allowance is made for the impact of future changes in these assumptions such as the increasing life expectancy of pensioners or for some industries the increasing turnover of employees, as these two assumptions in particular can have a noticeable impact on the scheme's funding level and future contribution rate.

Of greater significance, however, are the financial assumptions which cover the following:

1. Long-term investment return on assets.
2. Future increases in earnings as a consequence both of inflation and promotion.
3. Increases to pensions once in payment.
4. Rate of revaluation for deferred pensions up to the NPD.
5. Rate of increase in dividends.
6. Assumed notional investment portfolio.

It is not the absolute value of these assumptions but the difference between each one and the long-term investment return which is of importance: for example, an assumed long-term investment return of 9 per cent and a rate of increase in earnings of 7 per cent is effectively assuming a real rate of return over earnings of 2 per cent (9 − 7 per cent) and it is this real rate of return which has a significant impact on the valuation result.

You should discuss with the actuary the impact of these financial assumptions. How do they compare with other similar schemes? Why have changes been made since the last valuation? What would be the consequence of changing the assumptions on both the funding level and future contribution rate? It is important that the company is aware of the sensitivity of the actuary's calculations – which are basically part of a mathematical model – to changes in the assumptions. What are the consequences of using a more, or less, conservative set of assumptions (for example using a smaller or larger real rate of return over earnings)? Has the actuary included any margins or reserves within the assumptions? If so, what are they and what is the justification for their inclusion?

It must be remembered that the trustees must at all times bear in mind the security of members' benefits. They will therefore require a more cautious approach to funding than the company which will be looking at a 'best estimate' of the contribution rate and trying to avoid building up unnecessary surpluses. Getting this balance right between the interests of the members and those of (effectively) the shareholders is difficult and needs careful consideration. It is possible therefore to have one set of assumptions for use by the trustees in funding the scheme and a separate, less conservative set for use by the company in accounting for pension costs in accordance with Statement of Standard Accounting Practice Number 24 of the accountancy profession.

Your aim is to ensure that the actuary has full information regarding the company's employment policy and future plans – as far as they could impact upon the pension scheme – and that you understand and are comfortable with the method and main assumptions used by the actuary in his or her calculations. Furthermore you must ensure you are aware of the consequences of using one set of assumptions rather than another. Too conservative a set of assumptions can lead to unnecessary surplus within the scheme and potentially a lower profit for shareholders' interests. Too weak a set of assumptions can lead to a deficit within the scheme and the need to make additional cash injections into the scheme possibly at a time when the company's trading and cash flow positions are unsatisfactory.

A comparison of the assumptions with the scheme's actual experience can be revealing and give pointers to future trends. It is also valuable to analyse, in general terms, how the surplus or deficit has arisen since the last actuarial valuation. However, in all but the very large schemes a thorough analysis would be spurious.

9.3.3 Solvency

This is the term given to a snapshot view of the scheme at any particular time in the event of it being terminated and wound up. The aim is to determine whether the scheme assets – which will be the cash value of the assets as if they were all sold at that date – are sufficient at the effective date of calculation to provide members with their accrued benefits.

Normally the accrued benefits are pensions in payment, deferred pensions for those who have left service and the deferred pensions that would be payable to all current active members as if they left service at the date of calculation. The calculation would normally allow for the trustees' practice of providing discretionary increases to pensions once in payment, generous early retirement provisions (which may be subject to company agreement) and any augmentations. However these elements could be ignored and you should therefore determine what actually has been included in the benefit calculation.

The value of these benefit entitlements would often be the actuary's best estimate of the cost of buying them out with a life office on terms applicable at the effective date. However, for deferred pensioners and active employees it could be taken as the current 'cash equivalent' or transfer value.

Solvency is therefore very volatile as it varies with market conditions, particularly in relation to equity values and current interest rates which determine the cost of buying out benefits with life offices and the calculation of transfer values. It is perfectly possible to have a pension scheme which on an ongoing ('going concern') basis is well funded and 'on target' to provide the benefits as promised, but because of the short-term volatile nature of stock markets and interest rates could technically be insolvent. This is not normally a problem unless the company has serious trading problems itself and is likely to cease trading – and in this situation it is unlikely to have any surplus cash to pay into the pension scheme to remedy the problem. Running a pension scheme merely to cover the solvency position is clearly a very dangerous approach for both the members and the company. In normal circumstances the actuary's funding method and assumptions will have built a notional reserve or buffer into the funding to ensure the scheme is always solvent.

As a company you should be aware as far as possible of the solvency position, its volatility and the circumstances in which it could be serious. Forewarned is forearmed: there is little worse than having unexpected, unpleasant surprises. The Goode Committee followed by the White Paper and subsequently the 1995 Pensions Act have made certain recommendations concerning minimum solvency and these are reviewed briefly in Chapter 12.

9.4 Surplus

There are different types of surplus depending on the circumstances which give rise to the calculation. There are also different amounts of surplus depending on the assumptions adopted by the actuary.

9.4.1 Funding surplus

This (or a deficit) arises as a consequence of the normal funding plan of the scheme and the triennial actuarial valuation. It is essentially a consequence of the method used and the scheme's short-term actual experience being different from the assumptions made by the actuary, which are essentially long-term. It is therefore quite possible for elements of surplus to arise at one valuation and disappear at the next. Funding surplus is therefore something which should be treated with care. It acts as a buffer to be used when the scheme's actual experience is adverse (for example when short-term investment returns have been lower than anticipated by the actuary or the increase in earnings has been higher than assumed). It enables the trustees to take a more aggressive approach to the investment strategy without jeopardising the basic security of members' benefits. It can be used to provide augmentations to members' benefits, for example in the case of hardship or special need, without the requirement of the company to make additional payments immediately. It can be used over time to provide discretionary increases to pensions in payment. Finally, and normally, it can be used by amortising over a period of years to stabilise or reduce company cost. When there is a deficit the reverse is true and the company will normally be expected to fund the deficit over a short period. Simply to assume that funding surplus should always be used to provide improvements to benefits is unsound because such surplus, by its very nature, can in the longer term be more illusory than real.

9.4.2 Statutory surplus

The Finance Act 1986 requires schemes to eliminate surplus in excess of a statutory level. The statutory level is determined using a statutory set of assumptions which are generally more conservative than those used by most schemes and therefore the scheme may have a large funding surplus without any statutory surplus. Any surplus of assets in excess of 105 per cent of the liabilities as calculated on the statutory basis must be eliminated by one of the following:

1. Benefit improvements.
2. A reduction in company and/or member contributions over a maximum of five years.
3. A refund of surplus to the company – but in this case increases at the rate of LPI must be granted to all current and future pensioners before any refund can be considered. The refund will then be subject to a 40 per cent tax charge.

From the company's point of view it is very rarely of benefit to build up a statutory surplus because of the controls and procedures that have to be followed should such a surplus exist. Therefore it is important to monitor the statutory surplus position, particularly for example where there are major redundancy exercises which could give rise to surplus or where short-term investment performance is exceptionally good, and take remedial action. Such action may be by means of contribution reduction to avoid having a statutory surplus rather than being required to use it in a way and at a time which are not suitable. (Statutory surplus is a special form of funding surplus.)

9.4.3 Winding-up surplus

Real surplus only exists when the scheme is being wound-up. The assets and liabilities are crystallised and the costs are known. Here the company, trustees and actuary work together to determine how the surplus should be allocated. The scheme rules will often be non-explicit and may leave the surplus to be allocated by the trustees on the advice of the actuary and with the agreement of the company. There are many permutations to consider and many different views on what is an equitable distribution. The actuary will provide guidance on the most suitable allocations. If the rules are explicit, they must of course be obeyed. The 1995 Pensions Act gives more power to the trustees than the company in this respect (see Chapter 12).

9.5 Transfer values

The concept of a transfer value has received a great deal of publicity, indeed one could say notoriety, in recent years. It arises as an expression of the cash sum which can be made available at the date of calculation in lieu of the benefits which would eventually emerge from the pension scheme. The automatic benefit under a defined benefit scheme is a pension from NPD, the transfer value being an option available as an alternative. The actuary decides on a rate, or rates, of interest (and other financial assumptions) at which to make the calculations, allows for the probability of each payment being made, and totals the sum of all the separate potential payments.

Since future investment returns are uncertain, there is plenty of scope for difference of opinion about the rate of interest to be used in the calculation. Hence there is a range of variation between transfer values representing the same benefits. Curious as it may seem, there is much greater uniformity in the assumptions about the probabilities of the separate payments being made.

Transfer values between employers' pension schemes had been available on a voluntary basis for many years. However, they really came to prominence following the 1985 and 1986 Social Security Acts. The then government regarded both freedom of choice and full portability as essential to the pensions system. As a result the business of transfer values has become a major industry in its own right. Members leaving schemes now have the right to take their transfer value to a personal pension or to their next employer's scheme. However, in moving to a personal pension the nature of the contract completely changes.

In most pension scheme trust deeds and rules it is the trustees who determine the actual amount of transfer value to be paid based on the advice of the actuary. The actuary can take a more optimistic or pessimistic view of current and future investment returns and therefore recommend lower or higher transfer values respectively. However, the choice of transfer value basis can have an impact not simply on the individual leaver's eventual benefit but also on the scheme's solvency, as we have seen earlier, and it is therefore important that the company is also aware of the approach the actuary is taking in the determination of transfer values.

The actuary must follow mandatory requirements set by the Institute and Faculty of Actuaries in establishing the transfer value basis to be adopted. However these requirements permit a wide range of possibilities and efforts are now being made to condense the range of possible alternatives.

In determining the benefits which can be purchased in your scheme by a transfer value being paid from another scheme the actuary is required to use the same basis as for transfers out, thereby ensuring consistency of treatment in this respect.

9.6 Other considerations

In most defined benefit schemes options are provided to members, such as the following:

1. Early retirement.
2. Late retirement.
3. Tax-free cash instead of pension.
4. Conversion of member's pension to a spouse's pension.

Such options can be financially neutral to the scheme or may imply an additional cost (or reduced cost). In setting up the scheme the company should consider its attitude to these options and discuss the best approach with the actuary. The impact on the contribution rate of such options is normally not significant but where for example the company is undertaking a major early retirement exercise as part of a redundancy programme the impact on a scheme's funding level and future contribution rate can be significant.

From time to time a company will wish to augment a member's benefits and will need to know the cost of such an augmentation and whether there is a need to make any immediate payment to the scheme. (This latter aspect is usually a trustee decision.) Where the augmentation is large the actuary will consider the impact on the funding level, solvency and contribution rate. As a consequence of these considerations he or she will advise whether the augmentation cost should be paid immediately, can be spread over a short period of years or can be provided out of surplus and become an adjustment in the future contribution rate from the next valuation. The impact of augmentations and, for example, making bonuses pensionable can be significant and it is therefore very important that the company keeps the actuary informed of its intentions and requests costing implications before giving any commitment. This is particularly the case in recruiting senior individuals when all too often a promise is made to match previous benefits only to find after the event that there is an immediate and significant pension cost – particularly where there is only a relatively short period of years over which to fund for such benefits.

General benefit improvements are considered from time to time as a consequence of negotiation with members or of legislative change, and the best time to consider the costs of such improvements is when the actuary is already doing the triennial actuarial valuation. In all these matters it is important to remember that in pensions terms any salary increases and many benefit improvements and augmentations have an impact on the benefits that have accrued to date as well as those accruing over the member's future working life. For example, for a man earning £30,000 who is close to his normal retirement date and has accrued a two-thirds pension, a salary increase of 10 per cent increases the company's payroll cost by £3,000 (ignoring NI contributions, etc.). The increase in his pension would be £2,000 (i.e. two thirds of 10 per cent of £30,000) but the cost of that could be over £20,000 and if the scheme is not adequately funded the £20,000 cost may be required to be paid immediately.

Talking to your actuary in advance of making the commitment is therefore very important.

Checklist 9   Paying for the benefits

Actuarial valuation
- funding method
- demographic assumptions
- financial assumptions
- funding level and solvency
- impact of change in assumptions
- cautious or incautious

Surplus
- funding surplus
- statutory surplus
- winding-up surplus

Options
- transfer values
- early retirement
- cash commutation
- conversion rate to spouse's pension

Company
- SSAP24 figures
- amortising surplus or deficit
- does actuary know and understand company's situation and future plans?

10 Audit and review

Every business has customers. So does every pension scheme – they are the beneficiaries. This includes the company, for two reasons. It benefits from the goodwill generated by the pension scheme and the company is often the remainderman in any distribution of surplus, particularly in the event of the winding-up of the scheme.

You will normally keep in touch with your customers, ensuring that they are provided with a good product and after-sales service. They will give you feedback – particularly if it is critical – and you will want to take steps to ensure that you keep them happy with a quality product which they value. It must be reliable, easily understood, satisfy your customers' particular needs and provide a comfort factor so they come back for more. The customer is always right!

Do you look after your pensions customers in the same way? Does the scheme satisfy their needs and yours? Are they aware of the value of the benefits? Are you keeping an eye on the running of the scheme to ensure adequate security, value for money from contributions and from advisers and an efficient operation as far as the day-to-day running of the scheme is concerned? An audit or review should not simply be left until you consider changing benefits. Just as the company strives to reduce costs, to increase revenues and to improve product quality so the same processes should be adopted within the pension scheme which from one point of view can be considered as a financial subsidiary of the company – with obvious restrictions and controls.

So where do you start? The answer is probably to look at your organisation and review the changes that have taken place over the last few years in its business direction. This will have impacted upon the operational structures within the business and also the recruitment and employment policies. Have the type and style of workforce changed or are they likely to be changing in the near future? If so, what are the changes: more temporary workers or part-timers? Is there more overtime or piece work? Do you encourage fixed contract work? Are there more single or single-parent employees on your workforce? A simple review of the items will lead you to consider whether or not you would benefit from a survey of employees and their needs. The days of the married male breadwinner with 2.4 children are fast disappearing.

Having identified these potential changes the next stage is to consider the impact of these on the benefits provided and whether or not members perceive the benefits you as a company are providing as being of value. The perceived value of any benefits provided to employees is very important. If they do not consider the benefits provided as being of value, either the benefits are unsuitable to their changing needs or the communication of such benefits is lacking. Either way you have a problem and as an organisation you are not deriving the goodwill and value you had hoped for.

Therefore the aim of your review is perhaps twofold:

1. To identify whether you are getting value for money from the company's contributions to the pension scheme.
2. To ensure that the scheme is being run efficiently with adequate safeguards for the interests of all beneficiaries.

Your role in such a review is to get a better feel of how everything fits together and is operating. Should you find that you need more than a superficial review or greater analysis of some of the workings of the scheme and its structures you will inevitably call for expert help, either from your existing consultants or perhaps a second opinion which can often be a refreshing approach.

The main areas for review are therefore as follows:

1. Scheme benefit structure.
2. General adminisration.
3. Communication and disclosure.
4. Documentation and balance of power.
5. Funding, finance and investment.
6. Trustees' effectiveness.

The aim of this book and more particularly this chapter is not to turn you into an expert but to give you some things to think about and encourage you to ask more pertinent questions of your advisers. Many of the aspects of a review are considered elsewhere in the book and this chapter will therefore only highlight the main items to be considered.

10.1 Scheme benefit structure

We have moved on from the days when only married men with 2.4 children were employed. There are now many more employees who are either single or single-parent families or perhaps with financial dependants. There may be employees with single-sex relationships. What, if any, provision is made for their dependants? Are children's or orphans' benefits provided on the death of the member or only on the second death of the member and spouse? This would be not a lot of help to single-parent families but presumably the rules of the scheme give the trustees some discretion in such a situation.

This may be the case in a defined benefit scheme where there is a fund for the trustees to use. That particular flexibility may not be available in the normal defined contribution scheme.

How many of your employees actually retire from the company? Now-adays the average employee has three to four jobs before retiring. The changing nature of your work may place greater emphasis on short-term contracts or a higher turnover of employees after three to five years as we become more dependent on 'high-tech' solutions to business problems. Such job mobility often brings with it the desire for flexible solutions to pensions either via a personal pension or a defined contribution scheme or a combination of basic core benefits with a choice of additional benefits depending on the employees' needs.

The variety of differing employees' needs means that all too often the benefit structure of the pension scheme is a compromise solution which does not satisfy anyone. If there is a demand for greater variety then flexible benefits may be the answer, not simply on the pensions side but covering all parts of the employee's remuneration package. By providing base core benefits and a wide choice of add-ons you can satisfy the needs of most employees without massively increasing either administrative complexity or cost.

There has in recent years been an encouragement from the Government to move towards more variable pay reflecting the profitability of the organisation and the efforts of employees giving rise to the profits. The introduction of profit-related pay and other bonus schemes could well have introduced a variability into pensionable earnings leading to less certainty regarding the final salary benefit being promised. The total remuneration package is sometimes altered and distorted by piecemeal changes and it can be useful to review pensions as part of the total remuneration package.

Changing government attitudes towards social security will also have an impact. If for example you operate a benefit structure with a target pension which incorporates state benefits then reducing state benefits increases the burden on the scheme and company costs.

Whether to have defined benefit or defined contribution is a point that is regularly raised. The finance director, particularly in small and medium-sized companies, is perhaps all too frequently swayed by the controllable cost aspects of the defined contribution approach. The loss of flexibility in funding and the loss of participation in scheme surplus can be counter arguments but by far the most important aspect is the benefit to the members. During their working lives a straightforward defined contribution approach is more easily understood and appreciated, particularly by the short-service employee. It is only when retirement is close at hand and interest rates low that the member realises that his or her pension pot is not as valuable as once thought. Schemes can be designed to avoid the worst aspect of both defined contribution and defined benefit and still have a controllable cost.

10.2 General administration

The administration service you provide to your members (the customers) is crucial. The company payroll and personnel functions have to interface with the pensions administrator (whether internal or external). Any review should look very carefully at the information flow to the pensions administration unit before reviewing the unit itself. Response times and standards should have been set from the outset. The review will look at performance against standards. Have there been any noticeable delays? If so, what is the reason?

Most of the correspondence with members will be on standard letters. Are they clear and do they inform and promote the scheme? Have you seen them and made suggestions for the trustees to consider?

The process of review is often best conducted by following different members' progress through the scheme year. New entrants, deaths, early leavers, retirements and benefit statements can then be considered separately with the administrators and compared with the timescales set.

There can be times when the information provided by the administrators to members is inaccurate either because information is incorrect or incomplete or because the benefit structure has changed but the administrators have not yet implemented all those changes.

A useful check can be a review of the basic definitions of scheme benefits. One can on occasions discover that perhaps the payroll department does not fully understand the definition of pensionable salary or that personnel are not implementing the eligibility conditions correctly. This often happens when new people are involved in the running of the scheme, and a short period of training and follow-up can avoid future problems. The data information flow through the different departments of your company which have any involvement in pensions can benefit from review to ensure there are no misunderstandings and that current procedures do not create delays.

10.2.1 Communication and disclosure

The requirements of the Disclosure of Information Regulations and the suggestions from the Goode Committee are in the main good practice. Some items, however, are far more important than others as far as member communication is concerned. Good communication enhances the value and reputation of the scheme. Unfortunately the opposite is true for poor communication and this can also lead to very expensive rewrites. Obviously all items of information sent to members should be reviewed for consistency and to ensure that the correct message is sent. It is not suggested that the company should adversely interfere with what is essentially a trustee matter in terms of disclosure. However, the scheme is a partnership in which the company has a need to communicate to members about the benefits under the scheme and its involvement in the scheme. Probably the three main items for disclosure are the scheme booklet, the trustees' report (the members' version) and members' annual benefit statements. All too often the scheme booklet is out of date. With so many changes in practice, legislation and benefit design this is quite understandable, but how often are updating inserts provided, particularly for new entrants? Existing members will normally have been provided with announcements when any changes are introduced and at the very least such announcements should be included with the printed booklet for new entrants. How much better it is if new entrants get an up-to-date booklet or at least are given a summary of benefit changes since the booklet was last produced rather than a series of formal announcements. Are the booklet and announcements clear and do they give examples of how members' benefits are determined in a simple readable manner? Even nowadays reference to the earnings cap in scheme booklets is limited. Remember that some of your new employees today may be subject to the cap in twenty years' time (particularly those who are fast track middle management). There is a need to establish company policy towards the cap and to notify all members of that policy if you do not wish to build up potential problems (both financial and personnel) for the future.

10.2.2 Documentation and balance of powers

Rules need to be constantly updated. Do the calculation of benefits and the members' booklet agree with the rules? Is the scheme run in accordance with the rules or are there inconsistencies? How up to date are the rules and when were all the various amending deeds last consolidated? Errors and misunderstandings can occur as a consequence of having a series of amending deeds over several years which are not consolidated and are inadvertently overlooked. From time to time senior employees may be provided with additional pension benefits but sometimes such augmentations are not adequately documented and possibly are not even being funded for.

The scheme's balance of powers has been covered in Chapter 5. Where the trustees or company have exercised any of their powers under the pension scheme it is worthwhile investigating whether the correct procedures have been followed and the decisions made documented both in the company and trustees' minutes.

If your scheme is contracted-out, do you have a valid contracting-out certificate covering all the subsidiaries and employments which are covered by the scheme? It is all too easy to overlook the contracting-out formalities when a company acquires, loses or establishes a new subsidiary.

10.2.3 Funding, finance and investment

Any review should look objectively at the scheme's funding position and level of future contributions. Are there major differences between the contributions actually paid to the scheme and those allowed for in the accounts under Statement of Standard Accounting Practice Number 24 (SSAP24)? There often will be, but is there an understandable explanation or is too conservative an approach being taken on behalf of the trustees? Can a more realistic approach be adopted?

Are company and members' contributions paid on time? Indeed, is there a set date for paying company contributions? Do significant delays occur between payment of contributions and investment and if so why? Are the cash sums held by trustees earning interest on deposit or lying in a current account unnecessarily?

Do the auditors do a thorough job and is an audit report presented to the trustees and company? Has an investment strategy been set and followed? Has the investment risk profile always been acceptable? How successful have the various investment decisions been? Are the benchmarks and targets still appropriate and achievable? Has the performance been acceptable? Are the assets secure and in the name of the trustees? (You may wish to check this with those responsible for custodianship.) Have you checked the investment and custodianship fees? Are all the tax reclaims and payments up to date?

10.2.4 Trustees' effectiveness

For most schemes the company is involved in the appointment of at least some of the trustees and gives them instructions on how to run the scheme as detailed in the scheme rules. So, how are they doing? If as a company you operate an employee appraisal system, do you appraise the trustees – either separately or as a group? Do they have regular meetings and is their performance, in all their areas of responsibility, satisfactory? On appointment were they given any guidance or training? Some may not even have a copy of the scheme rules!

10.3 Conclusion

There are no checklists at the end of this chapter as they are provided in other chapters. The audit and review must be a process of fact finding, identifying blockages in the process and inefficiencies where improvements can be made. It is a process of updating and education and will be constructed differently for each scheme. Should you require a more in-depth review, then your professional advisers should be involved.

D Current topics and future implications

In this section we devote one whole chapter to the earnings cap and implications for future benefit design. The second chapter deals with sex equality, the impact of the Goode Committee, the Government's White Paper and the 1995 Pensions Act. Before embarking on any new benefit design, such issues, however uncertain their final outcome, must be considered.

11 The earnings cap

11.1 What is the earnings cap?

The emphasis in other chapters in this book has been on 'approved' schemes. The 'approval' referred to is that of the Inland Revenue and it is sought in order to obtain the very valuable tax concessions which are granted to encourage retirement provision. However, the Finance Act 1989 introduced a new concept to the United Kingdom: that of the 'earnings cap', and with it the 'unapproved pension scheme'.

The earnings cap is a limit placed on the earnings which can be taken into account in calculating the maximum benefits which can be provided from an approved retirement benefits scheme. It applies to all new members joining existing approved schemes on or after 1 June 1989 and all members of new schemes established on or after 14 March 1989. This means that if an individual changes employer on or after 1 June 1989 he or she will be subject to the earnings cap when he or she joins the new employer's approved scheme. Apart from affecting the maximum benefits which can be taken from an approved scheme, members' own contributions to approved schemes are limited to 15 per cent of the earnings cap. There are transitional provisions to avoid the rule being applied unfairly, such as when the employer replaces an existing scheme to which the cap did not apply, or where an employee is promoted and becomes a member of another scheme of the same employer.

The earnings cap also applies to contributions payable to PP arrangements in any tax year starting after 5 April 1989, with the maximum contributions percentages being based on the earnings cap. However, the earnings cap does not apply to RACs which are approved under Sections 620/621 of the Taxes Act 1988 (formerly approved under Section 226 or 226A of the Income and Corporation Taxes Act 1970), although as these policies had to be in force before 1 July 1988 this concession will eventually be eliminated as the policyholders retire.

The cap was set at £60,000 for the tax year 1989/90 and was to increase each year in line with increases in the RPI (rounded up to the nearest £600). The linking has been applied ever since, with the exception of the tax year 1993/94 when it was frozen at the 1992/93 level of £75,000. The linking was restored in 1994/95 when the limit became £76,800.

11.1.1 The significance of the earnings cap

At the moment it is tempting to dismiss the earnings cap as a problem only for senior executives of large companies, but to take this attitude would be a serious mistake. Over the years earnings have traditionally increased on average faster than the RPI. This means that the limit will gradually reduce in terms of earnings levels. For example, if earnings increase by 2 per cent per annum faster than the RPI, by the year 2020 the earnings cap will apply to all those earning £47,000 or more at 1994 price levels. The problem of providing retirement benefits in a tax-efficient manner is going to be an ever-growing one. In addition, the precedent set by the freezing of the cap over 1993/94 does not bode well for the future. In the United States of America a similar cap concept was introduced in 1974. Until 1982 that, too, was indexed to price inflation. However in 1982 Congress decided to reduce the level it had then reached. How long will it be before a government in the United Kingdom follows suit?

The story, however, is not one of unmitigated bad news. Introduced together with the cap was the concept of 'unapproved' pension schemes. Prior to April 1989 it was not possible to mix approved and unapproved arrangements in respect of the same employment. In order to make full use of the tax concessions available, an approved scheme would have to be established. This would be subject to the appropriate limits. The maximum benefit limits under occupational schemes took into account any benefits arising in respect of the employment which were provided by other arrangements, whether approved or unapproved. In addition, the tax legislation at the time subjected an individual to income tax on the notional value of any unapproved benefits to which he or she was prospectively entitled. This meant that the individual was liable to pay income tax on a benefit he or she had not received and had no prospect of receiving for many years. The effect of all this was therefore to place a limit on the amount of retirement income which any individual could receive in respect of employment, albeit that the limit was calculated as a percentage of the remuneration received while in employment, rather than being fixed to a monetary level applied uniformly across all employees.

The 1989 legislation introduced a relaxation which means that employers can now provide whatever level of benefits they wish, albeit without the tax advantages of an approved scheme. This gives the employer greater flexibility in that benefits can be provided:

1. Without being restricted by the earnings cap.
2. Without being restricted by the two-thirds maximum pension allowed in approved schemes.
3. With no restriction on benefits for short service.

This whole area of benefit provision is still very much in its infancy. It is extremely complicated, relying on the interaction of a number of existing legislative provisions, together with piecemeal amendments introduced in 1989 and subsequently. The full implications of preservation, equal access, cash equivalents and statutory revaluation on unapproved schemes is not yet settled. Few practitioners and advisers have a proper understanding of all the considerable complications involved. Consequently many employers have introduced inappropriate arrangements for employees who are subject to the earnings cap. This chapter provides a limited guide through the maze, but is not a substitute for individual advice, taking account of the circumstances of each particular situation. However, before we consider how to approach retirement planning using unapproved schemes, we need to spend some time looking at the types of scheme available.

11.2 Unapproved retirement benefits schemes

An unapproved scheme must be a 'retirement benefits scheme' to come within the new regime. This is defined in Section 611 of the Income and Corporation Taxes Act 1988 ('Taxes Act'). It means essentially any arrangement which provides benefits for employees or their families which includes 'relevant benefits'.

'Relevant benefits' in turn are defined in Section 612 of the Taxes Act. They include a pension, lump sum, gratuity or similar payment which is payable under the following conditions:

1. When an employee or former employee retires or dies.
2. In anticipation of retirement.
3. After a person has retired or died (in recognition of past service).
4. As compensation for any change in the conditions of continuing employment.

Accident benefits, redundancy payments and other payments for termination of service do not normally fall within the definition of relevant benefits.

An unapproved retirement benefits scheme is any retirement benefits scheme which has not been approved under Part XIV Chapters I (Occupational Schemes) or IV (Personal Pension Arrangements) of the Taxes Act. It does not have to adopt any particular form or structure. Any decision, however informal, to provide a relevant benefit is sufficient to constitute an unapproved scheme. However, it is normal to set up more formal arrangements, for example through the contract of employment or a formal trust deed. Such an arrangement can cover one employee or a group of employees.

In practice, unapproved schemes can be divided into two types:

1. Unfunded schemes under which no assets are set aside to meet the benefits which are paid from the employer's resources on a pay-as-you-go basis as they fall due.

2. Funded schemes under which assets are set aside to meet the benefits promised.

The sections below look at the differences between the unfunded and funded approaches. The tax treatment of such schemes is summarised in Table 11.1 before being considered in more detail. Table 11.1 helps to illustrate the different considerations that should be taken into account in establishing unapproved schemes.

11.3 Unfunded unapproved retirement benefits schemes (UURBS)

An UURBS is essentially a promise by an employer to pay an employee, or dependants, benefits which include relevant benefits. The employer cannot make any payments or formally allocate any assets to meet the promise as that would change the scheme from an unfunded to a funded one.

11.3.1 The advantages of UURBS

1. The employer does not have to set up any formal arrangement. The usual approach is for the benefits promise to be contained in the employee's contract of employment or in a letter qualifying the contract.
2. The employer can provide the employee with exactly the same pension and spouse's pension as if he or she had not been subject to the earnings cap.
3. Meanwhile the employer has the use of the money which would otherwise have been paid to a pension scheme to fund the benefits promised.
4. The employee is in exactly the same tax position as if the pensions were being provided under an approved scheme. There is no tax charge to the employee while the benefit is accruing and the pensions are taxed in payment as income in the same way as those from an approved scheme.
5. The amount of the pension is not subject to any limits other than those imposed by the employer.
6. The whole or any part of the pension can be commuted for a lump sum. The lump sum is taxable in the year it is received.

11.3.2 The disadvantages of UURBS

1. The employer receives no Corporation Tax relief at the time of reserving funds, and the reserve rolls up net of Corporation Tax. In addition, unless the pension is secured through an insurance policy or other arrangement when the employee retires, the commitment remains on the employer's balance sheet. Similarly a commitment is retained in

Table 11.1 Tax treatment of retirement benefit schemes

	Exempt approved retirement benefits scheme	Unapproved unfunded retirement benefits scheme	Funded unapproved retirement benefits scheme
Contributions			
Employee	Fully tax deductible up to 15% of pay (subject to the cap)	Not applicable	No tax relief
Employer	Fully deductible as expense for tax purposes in year of payment	Fully deductible as an expense when a payment is finally made	Fully deductible in year of payment
	Not taxable as income of employee	Not taxed as income of employee provided no earmarked assets	Taxed as income of employee in year of payment
	No NI contributions	No NI contributions	NI contributions payable on amounts paid to employee to meet tax or paid direct to Inland Revenue to meet tax liability
Investment	All investment income and capital gains free of UK tax	All earnings subject to corporation tax	Trust taxed at basic rate with trust capital gains tax exemption provided that only relevant benefits are provided under the trust
Retirement benefits			
Pension	Taxed as earned income	Taxed as earned income	Taxed as earned income
Lump sum	Tax-free up to $1\frac{1}{2}$ final remuneration (subject to the cap)	Taxed in year of receipt	Tax-free
Death benefits			
Widow's pension	Taxed as earned income	Taxed as earned income	Taxed as earned income
Lump sum	Not usually subject to income tax or inheritance tax	Subject to income tax; no inheritance tax if estate not a possible beneficiary	Not usually subject to income tax or inheritance tax

respect of employees who leave service. The transfer of an accrued unapproved liability is difficult and employers may feel aggrieved at having to retain a balance sheet liability for someone who no longer contributes to the business.

2. The major disadvantage from the employee's viewpoint is the lack of security. The employer may become insolvent and unable to meet the pension payments when they eventually fall due. As assets cannot be set aside, the employee is in the same position as any other unsecured creditor. Alternatively the employer may come under new management and fail to honour the promise. As the pension promise could take twenty or thirty years to fulfil, such fears are not unreasonable.

3. Dependants also lack effective protection. They may not be able to enforce a broken pension promise through the employment contract, since they were not party to it. The lack of a trust also robs them of the usual remedies available to members of other types of pension schemes, although the UURBS can be established under trust.

4. At present it is not possible to obtain insurance against loss of the benefits. However, such insurance is generally available in the United States and may become available in the United Kingdom soon.

11.3.3 Normal pension age

As UURBS are not subject to any tax regulation, retirement can be at any age. However, to limit the cost and to enable the employer to ensure an orderly retirement in accordance with the needs of the business the pension age is normally the same as under the employer's approved pension scheme.

11.3.4 Final salary promise

1. The majority of UURBS provide a pension from normal pension age equal to a percentage of final salary for each year of service *less* the pension value of any benefits payable from approved schemes.

2. There is no limit on the annual accrual rate other than that imposed by the employer.

3. The pension can be at a flat rate or increasing at a specified rate or at the employer's discretion.

4. The employer can include a provision for part or all of the pension to be commuted for a lump sum or express the benefit partly as a pension and partly as a lump sum.

5. Both pensions and lump sums are taxed as income of the employee in the year of receipt.

6. A spouse's pension payable on the death of the employee can be included in the benefit promise.

11.3.5 Money purchase benefits

1. An UURBS can provide benefits which accrue in a similar manner to money purchase benefits in funded schemes. The employee's account is credited with the agreed contributions and a notional investment return is added. The total is the amount which the employer becomes liable to make available to provide the employee's benefits.
2. The benefits can be paid as a pension or a lump sum. The amount of the pension is normally calculated actuarially depending on whether the employee wishes to have a flat pension or one which increases during payment.

    A spouse's pension at retirement can be included as a required or optional benefit.

11.3.6 Early retirement

1. Here again the employer has total flexibility but in practice the options will be limited for the same reasons as affect the choice of normal pension age.
2. Final salary pension benefits are normally reduced to reflect both the shorter period of service and the longer period for which the pension is payable. If the benefits are mirroring the employer's approved pension scheme the same early retirement factors are normally appropriate.
3. If a money purchase approach is being used, the factors used to convert the employee's account balance to a pension will normally reflect his or her age at retirement.

11.3.7 Leaving service

Deferred pension

Although there are no tax rules governing the benefits from an UURBS the preservation regulations do apply to unapproved schemes. This is not normally a problem as the leaving service benefit is usually expressed as a deferred pension payable from the normal pension age equal to the pension accrued to the date of leaving. The benefits could of course be more generous, for example, as part of a leaving service settlement.

Transfer value

Theoretically a transfer to another unapproved pension scheme should be available. However, as this would result in the employee becoming immediately liable to tax on the amount transferred, this is not a practical option. It can best be dealt with by giving the employer the option to pay a transfer subject to the employee's agreement. The employee could have the option to have part of the transfer value paid directly. Any direct payment would be subject to a deduction for tax. However, the exercise of this option should be subject to the employer's agreement as otherwise an employee may elect to leave service prematurely in order to gain immediate access to the lump sum. The employer may also wish to include the right to deduct any NI contributions for which either the employee or the employer is liable on these payments.

Under the law and practice at the time of publication the liability for NI contributions only arises on the payment direct to the member. If the employee's earnings in the tax year have already exceeded the UEL the only cost in practice will be the 10.2 per cent employer's contributions on the direct payment.

11.3.8 Death-in-service benefits

Spouse's and dependants' pensions

Spouse's and dependants' pensions can be provided as part of the benefit promise. The level is entirely at the employer's discretion and does not have to be linked to the level of the employee's pension.

If the employer insures this benefit the employee will be taxed on the amount of the premiums. The beneficiary will also be taxed on any pension arising from the policy. Essentially, this will have changed the benefit from an unfunded to a funded unapproved one.

Lump sum

A lump sum can be paid to an employee's dependants from an UURBS. However, as the recipients will be liable to tax on the amounts paid to them it is usual to fund this benefit through an insurance policy and set it up under trust.

11.3.9 Financing the UURBS

A book reserve

As no assets can be allocated to meet the accruing liability under the benefit promise it is usual to establish a reserve in the employer's accounts. (For those employers subject to SSAP24 the reserve will form part of the SSAP24 reporting requirements.) The amount of the reserve is normally established using actuarial techniques similar to those used to fund an approved pension scheme but allowing for the tax implications.

Unallocated assets

Although no assets can be allocated specifically to meet the liability of the UURBS most employers recognise the need to have liquid resources available to pay the benefits as they arise. For this purpose they normally accrue reserves of cash or other easily realised assets. This approach avoids any cash-flow strains when the benefits fall due, particularly if part of the benefits will be paid as a lump sum rather than a pension.

Insurance

The employer cannot insure the benefits or the premiums become taxable income of the employee and the scheme is no longer an unfunded one. However, the employee may be able to insure against non-performance of the employer under his or her contract of employment. If the premiums are not paid from the employee's own resources, they too will become a taxable benefit. (The employee's salary could instead of course be increased appropriately.) The insurers will require the promise to pay the benefits to be a formal one and in a format acceptable to them.

At the time of writing the first such contracts are still at the development stage.

11.3.10 Employee contributions

An employee cannot contribute to an UURBS. However, an employee's income can be adjusted to allow for any contributions which would have been payable under the employer's approved scheme. From the employee's point of view, this is not a good idea because of lack of security. It would be bad enough for an employee to lose a benefit promised by the employer but infinitely worse to lose a benefit for which he or she had paid!

11.3.11 Incentive schemes

An UURBS can in certain circumstances be used as a vehicle for a long-term incentive scheme. The credits to the employee's account could be dependent on the company's profitability as could the notional investment return.

11.4 Funded unapproved retirement benefits schemes (FURBS)

A FURBS is any fund, scheme or arrangement which is not an approved retirement benefits scheme and to which an employer allocates assets to provide benefits which include relevant benefits. It is normally set up under a trust because of the following:

1. The assets of the trust are clearly separated from those of the employer. As the employees will have paid tax on the contributions to the trust it is desirable that they have clearly identified assets.
2. If the rules of the trust limit the benefits which can be provided from the trust to relevant benefits the investment income and capital gains accruing within the trust are taxed at the basic trustee rate of tax (25 per cent in 1994/95) rather than at the employee's marginal rate of tax.
3. The benefits paid under discretionary trust to an employee's dependants on his or her death should be free from inheritance tax provided that the employee's estate is not a possible beneficiary of the trust.

11.4.1 Advantages of a FURBS

1. The contributions paid to a FURBS are not subject to NI contributions by the employer or the employee.
2. If the FURBS provides only relevant benefits the investment income and capital gains of the trust are taxed at a favourable rate.
3. Any lump sum benefit payable from the FURBS is tax-free and there is no Inland Revenue limit on the lump sum. This enables the employee to build capital.
4. The employer does not have a large liability building up in the accounts.
5. The employee has the same security as under an approved scheme.

11.4.2 Disadvantages of a FURBS

1. The employee is taxed on the amounts paid to the FURBS by the employer. (There is no tax relief on employees' contributions so they do not usually contribute.) However, given that tax is payable at some point in respect of all unapproved arrangements, it can be beneficial to have settled the tax liability at a known rate, rather than deferring it to an uncertain future.

    This means that either the employee has to meet the tax liability out of his or her own resources or the employer has to arrange for part of the amount available for contributions to the FURBS to be paid direct to the employee to enable his or her tax liability to be met. (This process is known as 'grossing-up'.)

    The Inland Revenue will allow grossing-up arrangements whereby the tax on the amount paid to the FURBS is grossed-up and paid direct to the Inland Revenue. (Note, however, the Companies Act 1985 prohibits a company from paying a director's tax liability in this way.) However as NI contributions are payable on the amount paid to the Inland Revenue, there appears to be no real advantage in using the grossing-up approach.

The most advantageous approach is for the employee to nominate, before the payments become due, the amount which should be paid to the FURBS and the amount to be paid direct to him or her, subject to the employer's agreement.

2. There are administrative costs involved in running a FURBS which do not arise with an UURBS.

3. A FURBS is not suitable for funding final salary based pensions (but see below). Pensions from a FURBS are fully taxed despite the fact that tax was paid on the contributions. This makes it inappropriate to pay pensions from a FURBS – the benefits should be in the form of a lump sum.

    The cost of funding any specific level of benefits is likely to be higher in a FURBS than in an UURBS. This is because the monies set aside to fund the FURBS bear tax at the employee's marginal rate which will normally be 40 per cent at 1995 tax levels. This is higher than the highest corporation tax rate of 33 per cent which is effectively being levied on monies retained by the employer, i.e. the book reserve. Furthermore, the employee's marginal tax rate may be increased at any time, giving rise to even higher costs.

11.4.3 Common design features of FURBS

Because FURBS is not a suitable vehicle for funding final salary benefits it is normally used to provide benefits on a money purchase basis. However, as with any money purchase scheme, contribution rates can be established at the outset with the aim of meeting the cost at retirement of a given level of benefits.

When the FURBS is an alternative to the final salary UURBS, the member can make an election each year as to whether he or she wishes to accrue another year's benefits under the UURBS or to have an amount calculated by the employer's actuary made available for payment to a FURBS.

11.4.4 Normal retirement

It is usual to have the same NPD as in the employee's contract of employment. The benefit payable is the value of the employee's accrued account.

As there is a tax disadvantage in providing a spouse's pension through a FURBS (see below) they are normally provided by either of the following:

1. By a specific contribution to the employee's account to enable the employer to purchase an annuity contingent on the employee's death or give the spouse a part of the lump sum.

2. Through an UURBS set up alongside the FURBS with the spouse's pension being separately defined in the contract of employment or the additional agreement establishing the unapproved benefits.

11.4.5 Early retirement

As FURBS are normally set up on a money purchase basis, the benefits on early retirement are again normally the value of the member's accrued account.

11.4.6 Leaving service

The FURBS can include vesting provisions but as the employee has paid tax on the amount of the contributions the leaving service benefit is normally the value of the accrued account. However, to avoid the situation where employees leave service in order to obtain access to the lump sum it is usual for payment of the benefit to be deferred until the NPD or the earlier date at which an employee retires with the company's consent.

If the FURBS is being used to fund final salary benefits and the value of the employee's account is higher than the value of his or her leaving service benefit required by the preservation regulations, the excess can be retained in the FURBS to fund the benefits of another member, returned to the employer or the leaving member can be given more than required by preservation regulations. If he or she loses the benefit of the excess, the employee can claim a tax rebate and the employer will pay tax on any amount refunded. If the excess is retained in the FURBS, the member deemed to be benefiting will be taxed on it as though it were a direct contribution from the employer.

11.4.7 Death-in-service

1. A spouse's pension should not be provided from a FURBS as there is double taxation with both the pension and the contributions required to fund it being taxed.
2. A FURBS is an ideal vehicle for providing unapproved lump sum death benefits. The amounts payable from the trust should be payable to a range of beneficiaries at the discretion of the trustees. The beneficiaries should not include the employee's legal personal representatives (his or her estate) if the benefits are to be free of inheritance tax. These benefits are normally insured to avoid having to build up reserves which may not be required.

    Tax liabilities can arise if more than one employee is insured under the same insurance policy so the insurance policy covering the provision of unapproved lump sum death benefits should be an individual one covering only one employee and should not benefit from preferential premium rates obtained through the employer effecting other policies with the insurer.

3. The payment on the employee's death in service of the balance on his or her account to his or her beneficiaries may be subject to inheritance tax as part of the estate.

11.5 Retirement planning using unapproved schemes

How, then, should best use be made of unapproved arrangements? Maximum use should first be made of any spare capacity under tax-approved arrangements, whether they be an occupational scheme or through a personal pension arrangement. This may not be as easy as it sounds, since an employee's situation will need to be reviewed at least annually, to make sure that full use is being made of his or her current remuneration.

The difference between benefits from the approved arrangements and the total benefits promised should then be provided through an unapproved arrangement. The most flexible method is to build into the employee's contract of employment the facility for the employer to make notional contributions into an UURBS, whilst also setting up a FURBS alongside it. The employee is then given, on an annual basis, the choice as to how any contribution towards his or her retirement arrangements is to be allocated between the three types of arrangements. (Alternatively, he or she could, if personal circumstances and taxation conditions applicable at the time warrant, elect to have that year's contribution paid directly to him or her as a bonus, accepting that tax will be paid on it at the relevant marginal rate.)

The other matter which the employer must decide from outset is the level of that total contribution. In the early days of unapproved arrangements, many employers recruiting capped senior employees were apt to guarantee that the new recruit would receive retirement benefits at the same level as his or her uncapped colleagues. This meant, of course, that the employer became effectively responsible for bearing the cost of the employee's tax. In many cases this promise was made without thinking through the consequences, and many employers are now beginning to regret having made such a promise.

Arguably the best approach is to guarantee that the capped executive will have the same proportionate cost of the gross benefits made available to him or her, but that he or she is responsible for meeting any associated tax costs. This is a more logical approach and is consistent with the approach taken in respect of taxation borne by employees on other aspects of their remuneration package. Furthermore, the argument that there should not be a difference between the benefits received by senior employees doing the same job side by side, is based on a fallacy. In the short term, new recruits will indeed be worse off in net terms than their colleagues who have been with the employer for some time. However, as time goes by, a progressively larger proportion of the employees in that category will be subject to the earnings cap. Therefore within a relatively short period of time all the employees in that category will be subject to a comparable taxation basis. The employer will then find itself meeting the cost of employees' tax in a situation where the original rationale for such an expensive gesture has long since disappeared. By that time, it may be difficult to withdraw the benefit.

12 Live issues

Finally, what of the future? Will schemes designed today still be viable and appropriate in ten, twenty or forty years time? Leaving aside changing economic and cultural conditions, what legislative and other changes may be waiting around the corner to force change upon the way in which provision is made for retirement?

Since the all-party consensus was broken by the Conservative Government's radical changes in the 1980s, pensions have become a hot political issue. If it is correct to say that 'a week is a long time in politics', then any issue holding politicians' interests must be liable to sudden, frequent, and radical change. This is clearly incompatible with the stability required for an arrangement which may take forty years to prepare for its true purpose and which may then pay benefits for another twenty-five years or so. Yet that is the sort of environment in which schemes have had to work for the past decade and more.

It must be hoped that we will soon be entering a period of stability, but current signs suggest the opposite. This chapter 'flags' some of the current issues which promise to have a strong influence on retirement benefit provision over the next few years. After that, who can tell? The fact that there is so much uncertainty only serves to emphasise the need for constant reappraisal of the arrangements that are in force. Even the issues and solutions discussed in this book may be obsolete within a short time, which underlines the need to select a good adviser, as proposed in Chapter 3.

12.1 Equality between the sexes

The issue of equality between the sexes is today a major issue – not to say headache – for pension schemes. It has implications in many areas and the inequalities – whether actual or perceived – stem from two fundamental issues.

The first is the unequal retirement ages under the state pension schemes. Since early in the Second World War, the state schemes have been geared around retirement ages of 65 and 60 for men and women respectively. The earlier age for women was chosen as an encouragement and reward for women who were left alone at home while their husbands were away fighting for their country, and who consequently had to keep house, raise the children and work in the jobs left vacant by the departed men. Since the end of the war no government has had the strength of will to revisit the problem until finally forced by outside pressure to do so – but more of that later. In view of the importance of integrating the scheme benefits with those of the state schemes, occupational schemes have frequently adopted normal retirement ages of 65 and 60 for men and women respectively.

The second fundamental issue is that there is a significant difference between the life expectancies of the 'average' man and woman: the average woman lives some five years longer than her male counterpart (despite coping with the extra rigours of life identified earlier by Parliament!). This clearly has an effect on the cost of providing benefits which are paid by instalments until death, and on ascertaining the capital value of such benefits. This makes the somewhat simplistic aim of equalising the monetary amounts of contributions and benefits in respect of men and women effectively impossible to achieve.

The contortions which pension schemes have had to undertake as a result of both of these issues has caused a massive – and some would say wholly wasteful – expenditure of money and effort. The problems are still far from being settled, and this area looks set to remain 'live' for some time to come. Readers therefore need to understand the issues involved. (Note that in the examples which follow, it is assumed that the 'standard' normal retirement age is 65 for men and 60 for women although many schemes have by now equalised.)

The Social Security Pensions Act 1975 was the first piece of pensions legislation to refer to equality of the sexes (now re-enacted in Section 118 of the Pension Schemes Act 1993). It required that men and women doing similar work should have 'equal access' to their employer's scheme, i.e. they should be able to join on the same terms, at the same age and after the same qualification period. This effectively applied certain principles of the existing UK employment law (and of European law as set out in the Treaty of Rome) concerning pay, terms and conditions. European law was subsequently to return to haunt UK pension schemes.

First, a number of European Court judgments, notably that in favour of Mrs Helen Marshall, established the principle that, even where a woman's 'retirement age' is earlier than that of an equivalent man, she may carry on working until the male retirement age. This was then incorporated into the Sex Discrimination Act 1986. The implications for pension schemes were not quite straightforward. Where a woman had been allowed to carry on working, say to age 62, her pension at age 60 would be increased by an (actuarial) factor, typically between 9 and 12 per cent per year, to allow for the later commencement of the pension. Companies providing pension schemes were faced with a dilemma: should this practice continue or should the late retiree simply accrue more pension?

For example, say Mrs Brown's pension at age 60 was

$$\frac{20}{60} \times £15,000 = £5,000 \text{ p.a.}$$

Increasing this by 9 per cent simple per year for two years (to age 62) would give a pension of £5,900 a year. If, during the extra two years, her salary increased to £16,500 her 'notional' accrued pension would be

$$\frac{22}{60} \times £16,500 = £6,050 \text{ p.a.}$$

Although this is better than £5,000 and, as an implication of the new European 'angle', she might justifiably claim the higher figure, two questions arose:

1. If her salary rose to only £15,500, her 'notional' accrued pension would be £5,683 a year. Would she now get the higher figure of £5,900 a year?
2. Was it not true that, by insisting on 'being a man' (retirement age 65) and then technically retiring early at 62, she should suffer the actuarial early retirement factor (a reduction of 5 per cent a year simple) ending with a pension of, say

$$85\% \times £6,050 = £5,143 \text{ p.a.?}$$

Solutions of both kinds and all manner of hybrids were tried – even within the same company. But worse was to come, and in this respect the principle of 'best of all possible worlds' proved potentially very expensive.

12.1.1 Barber, Ten Oever, Coloroll and others

Barber v. *Guardian Royal Exchange Assurance Group*

In 1985 Mr Barber was made redundant by the Guardian Royal Exchange insurance company. One aspect of the GRE's severance terms particularly upset him: he was 52 years old. Had he been a woman of the same age, he would have been allowed to draw an immediate pension but because GRE's pension scheme had different normal retirement ages (and related terms) for men and women, he had to wait and consequently his benefit was worth less.

He referred the matter to the UK Industrial Tribunal alleging unlawful discrimination on the grounds of sex but, as this aspect of equality was not directly covered by UK law, it was referred by the Court of Appeal to the European Court of Justice.

On 17 May 1990, the European Court confirmed that pensions did indeed count as deferred pay and that Mr Barber should consequently have been entitled to an immediate pension. Mr Barber himself had died in the meantime but the judgment was, at least, good news for Mrs Barber.

Unfortunately, the judgment was not made in English or, apparently, with a full appreciation of the different views adopted in the Community of when pension 'accrues' or at what point it 'vests' and cannot be removed. Various questions therefore remained incompletely answered. The first, and most worrying, of these concerned retrospection. The European Court judgment was stated to apply only from 17 May 1990. However, did that mean that it applied only to pension *earned* after 17 May 1990 or to earlier accrual, e.g. forever, back to the date of the Treaty of Rome, to Britain's accession, or when?

This and other questions raised by the judgment led to a whole series of cases from across Europe to identify and find answers to equality issues. Briefly, the main ones were as follows.

Gerardus Cornelius Ten Oever v. *Stichting Bedrijfspensioenfonds voor het Glazenwassers en Sachoonmaakbedrijf*

This resolved in late 1993 that only pension *earned* during service after 17 May 1990 must be subject to equal terms. It also established that survivors' (widows' and widowers') benefits must be provided on equal terms.

Neath v. *Hugh Steeper Ltd*

Apart from exploring the retrospection question from a different angle, Mr Neath's case essentially demanded that the same actuarial factors should apply in respect of both sexes in circumstances such as calculation of transfer values and 'commutation' of pension for tax-free cash. The Court ruled that it was only the benefit promise at retirement which constituted 'pay' for the purposes of European law and that it was therefore perfectly valid to use different factors for men and women.

This judgment, viewed by many as running contrary to the Court's earlier view that *all* aspects of pension provision should be on equal terms, may well be seen as fundamental in establishing that it is the benefit which constitutes the 'deferred pay' and not the means of providing it.

Birds Eye Walls v. *Roberts*

The Roberts case sought to establish whether it is illegal, where state pension ages for men and women are unequal (e.g., 65 and 60 as in the United Kingdom), for a scheme to pay a 'bridging pension' to a man retiring before age 65. The Court ruled that, where an anomaly in retirement income was the result of government action (or inaction), it was permissible to make up the difference from the scheme.

Bridging pensions are, consequently, acceptable in appropriate circumstances.

Smith v. *Avdel Systems*

In this case, pension ages were changed on 1 July 1991 from 60 for women and 65 for men to a common age of 65. Seventy-eight women employed by Avdel Systems Limited argued that the pension rights which they had built up to 17 May 1990 could be taken at age 60 without any early retirement reduction. The Advocate General of the European Court of Justice made the following comments in his formal Opinion:

1. There is nothing in European law preventing the equalisation of pension ages in respect of service before 17 May 1990 but women may have remedies under UK contract and trust law.
2. Pension rights accrued during the period 17 May 1990 to 1 July 1991 by both men and women at Avdel could be taken from age 60 without reduction.

Pension rights for employment between 17 May 1990 and any later date of equalisation should therefore be based on those of the advantaged sex.

Coloroll

The distribution of scheme assets in the Coloroll schemes (the company having gone into receivership) raised many questions which the trustees were unable to resolve in the light of the Barber judgment. However, the European Court has addressed a number of these and, at the time of writing, the major outstanding problem is in relation to buying-out annuities; should this be done on 'unisex terms' – the same rates for men and women?

The Barber affair came as something of a surprise, not least because men were suddenly given a green light to claiming more valuable benefits. Inequality in state retirement ages was at the core of the problem but the Government showed little inclination to remedy the situation by taking swift action. Schemes were therefore suddenly required to provide equalised pensions from a common retirement age while the state continued to discriminate by making men wait until age 65 to draw their old age pension.

12.1.2 Solutions to equalisation

The solutions available to sponsoring companies all involved treading a tightrope between equality requirements, employment law and cost. Some, more affluent, organisations chose to equalise retirement ages at 60. This is the expensive – but possibly trouble-free – solution, potentially adding 15 per cent to the employer's ongoing pension costs. At the cost saving end of the range, equalisation at 65 was selected by many companies, particularly in the financially hard pressed manufacturing sectors. The drawback here would be women who objected to their retirement being postponed by five years. Intermediate solutions, such as equality at age 62 or 63, might be cost neutral but still involve a worsening of female terms of employment.

A more elegant solution was to offer a 'flexible retirement age' either for all pension or only for that earned after 17 May 1990. Normal retirement ages would be set at 65 but employees might be allowed to retire with an unreduced pension at any time after age 60. The requirement for the employer's consent was essential under this option because, otherwise, the preservation regulations would interpret the option to retire earlier as a right, thereby regarding retirement ages as having been equalised at 60 (not 65!) and consequently enhancing the early leaving benefit in an artificial and unintended way.

Because of the lingering uncertainties of the situation, which lasted for over three years, employers and, to some extent, their consultants were reluctant to take action which might require subsequent correction or incur costs which might subsequently turn out to have been unnecessary. Some employers equalised terms for new employees on a different basis than for existing employees; some only equalised for new employees, yet others took no action at all, with the subsequent result that, for the period between 17 May 1990 and the date of equalisation men appear to be entitled, by default, to the better 'female' terms.

The Government finally announced its intention in November 1993 to equalise state pension ages. Women will eventually have to wait until they are 65 to draw a state pension – but the change will be phased in over ten years, beginning in 2010. Women born before 6 April 1950 will not be affected at all and the full 65 retirement age will first affect those who were born after 6 April 1955. Those aged between will have state pension age between 60 and 65, with application according to a sliding scale.

So the uncertainty regarding state pension ages has been removed. The change will, however, do little to simplify the process of occupational plan design as state benefits will remain discriminatory for another twenty years. Thus there will be differences because occupational schemes will have equalised normal retirement dates with immediate effect to comply with the European Court judgments, whereas state benefits (and GMPs provided by occupational schemes in place of foregone SERPS pension) will revolve around a pension age anywhere between 60 and 65, depending on the sex and date of birth of the individual.

The new concept for contracting-out post-1997 under the 1995 Pensions Act hopefully may take account of these continuing inequalities.

12.2 Inflation-proofing

The need to provide increases to pensions in payment has been largely recognised since the high inflation era of the 1970s, during which time many pensioners who had retired with what had seemed perfectly adequate pensions were reduced to a state of poverty. However, the huge costs involved in protecting against inflation deterred all but the most wealthy employers from making more than token gestures. The OPB produced a report – *Protecting Pensions: Safeguarding benefits in a changing environment*. Interestingly, this covered at least some of the ground subsequently researched at greater length by the Goode Committee.

One of its recommendations was that

employers and trustees should be strongly encouraged to guarantee pension increases in line with price increases up to a maximum of 5% a year. If they are not prepared to give such a guarantee, we suggest they should give pensioners the option, on financially neutral terms, of taking a reduced pension with guaranteed increases in line with price increases up to 5% a year.

They also recommended that, in the event of a scheme being wound-up, there should be legislation to require inflation proofing at this level on the members' deferred benefits insofar as a surplus existed.

In the period before the Social Security Secretary, then Tony Newton, received this report, the Chancellor, Nigel Lawson, had introduced regulations to control surplus in pension schemes and to levy tax on its release. The OPB's suggestion that surplus should be used, on a winding-up, to provide increases up to 5 per cent a year (now colloquially known as LPI) was, supposedly, in harmony with these 'surplus regulations'. Mr Newton's subsequent 1990 Social Security Act adopted not only the requirement to provide LPI out of surplus insofar as possible in the event of a winding-up but also a requirement for ongoing schemes to fund such increases for benefits already earned (including in payment and deferred pensions) out of excessive surplus disclosed at a valuation, before allowing refund of surplus to the employer. The Act went even further; it stated that after A-day (whose date has yet to be announced) pensions accrued in future under defined benefit schemes should carry full protection.

Coming virtually at the same time as the Barber equality dilemma, the joint cost implications for many defined benefit schemes were extremely worrying. Having said that equalisation of retirement ages (below age 65) could involve an employer in an additional 15 per cent on costs, the combined effect of equalisation and LPI on a typical scheme currently providing increases at 3 per cent per year could easily be an increase in total costs by up to one-third.

Against a UK pensions background in which evolutionary improvement had been traditional, the proposed imposition by government of a statutory benefit improvement came as a shock to sponsoring employers and advisers alike. Ironically, only 'good' employers would be subject to the resulting difficulties; those without any scheme at all would be unaffected – as, apparently, would those operating money purchase schemes where any statutory inflation-proofing appeared likely to be traded off against a lower initial pension, without cost implication.

LPI has been imposed on past service benefits in a number of schemes which are substantially in surplus (where there has been a winding-up, a reconstruction or simply a plan to refund surplus to the employer). It has been introduced by many of the larger schemes on future service accrual. The 1995 Pensions Act however now proposes that from 1997, LPI must be included for all future service accrual both under defined benefit and defined contribution schemes.

12.3 The Maxwell affair

In December 1991, the newspaper and publishing tycoon Robert Maxwell was drowned in suspicious circumstances off the Canary Islands. The aftermath of his death disclosed fraud on a massive scale, partly involving the use of huge sums 'borrowed' from pension schemes within the Mirror Group and Maxwell Communications, to support his businesses. Such frauds are not unknown; what made the Maxwell affair different was the scale of the missing funds, the number of pensioners left without income and the fact that this had happened in large companies in the public eye with supposedly proper trustee procedures, statutory and professional super-vision.

Official investigations began immediately. But the public outcry required other action and the Government duly responded, with the establishment of the Pension Law Review Committee, chaired by Professor Roy Goode. The opportunity was taken to look at the law governing pension schemes from a wider perspective, as the Committee's terms of reference indicate:

To review the framework of law and regulation within which occupational pension schemes operate, taking into account the rights and interests of scheme members, pensioners and employers; to consider in particular the status and ownership of occupational pension funds and the accountability and roles of trustees, fund managers, auditors and pension scheme advisers; and to make recommendations.

This is not the proper place to consider the nature of Maxwell's fraud but the Goode Committee's recommendations are outlined briefly in the next section.

In the immediate aftermath of the scandal one important piece of legislation was brought forward: the 'Debt on the Employer Regulations', introduced by the 1990 Social Security Act. These required that, in the event of a scheme being wound-up, any shortfall in the funds required to provide members with their leaving service entitlement would be a debt on the employer. In the case of an ongoing employer, this would involve topping up the benefit entitlement from company funds; in the more common circumstances of company insolvency, the pension fund would rank *pari passu* with other unsecured creditors. This legislation undoubtedly gives some small comfort to scheme members – but not total reassurance.

At the same time, however, it caused consternation in the actuarial profession about the solvency of 'thinly funded' schemes, particularly in circumstances where interest rates are low and buy-out with insurance companies is consequently expensive. The issue of a minimum solvency standard, largely overlooked for a number of years, had suddenly become 'live' again.

12.4 The Goode recommendations

At the end of September 1993, the Goode Committee reported, making 218 recommendations.

Many of the recommendations merely reinforce what is currently perceived to be 'best practice'. Here, however, is a summary of the main recommendations:

1. Trust law should continue to govern schemes, but with suitable amendment to protect members' rights. The trust is seen as particularly useful in separating the funds supporting benefit promises from the company's own assets.
2. There should be member representation on trustee boards where there are more than fifty scheme members:
    (a) one-third appointed by members in a defined benefit scheme;
    (b) two-thirds appointed by members in a defined contribution scheme.
    There should be no requirement for an independent trustee and there is no recommendation for compulsory trustee training.
3. There should be a single 'Regulator' with overall responsibility for the regulation of schemes. The OPB should consequently be disbanded, although the Inland Revenue's Pension Schemes Office should remain.
4. There should be a 'minimum solvency requirement' for all funded schemes introduced over a five year transition period. This should require that scheme assets cover the sum of cash equivalent transfer values for active and deferred members as well as the actual cost of securing pensions already in payment through the purchase of immediate annuities.

    The solvency requirement should be 100 per cent of this figure but there should be a base level of 90 per cent, below which an immediate injection of funds should be required. The trustees should be required to obtain the necessary funds from the employer and, if the situation is not remedied, the Regulator would step in to supervise appropriate measures – possibly including winding-up the scheme.

The actuarial profession should establish the basis for the requirement, at the same time standardising methodology and assumptions to ensure greater consistency. They should be required to give annual certificates covering solvency in addition to triennial funding valuations. (This has significant implications for future funding, volatility of results and the investment strategy.)

5. The regulation of surpluses should remain largely as at present. Refunds to the employer should only be allowed if authorised by the scheme documents and would be subject to the approval of the Regulator. Employers should continue to be permitted to take contribution holidays, subject to maintaining minimum solvency and schemes should have up to fifteen years to reduce excessive surpluses.

6. Disqualification from acting as a trustee should apply on grounds similar to those applicable to company directors. The Regulator should also have power to disqualify for other specified reasons. In particular, the scheme actuary and auditor should not be allowed to act as trustee and it should be good practice to exclude the administrator.

7. Employers should continue to have the right to wind-up schemes with a reasonable notice period.

8. Transfer values should be calculated on a basis no less favourable than that used for the minimum solvency requirement (but may be reduced if the solvency level is less than 100 per cent). Penalties should be imposed on the scheme administrators if, without good cause, a transfer value is not paid within a year.

9. Trustees should have an overriding right to decide certain matters, such as the appointment of professional advisers, and, in conjunction with the employer, should decide investment strategy and the distribution of any unallocated surplus on winding-up.

A code of good practice should be laid down for trustees' meetings. Decisions should be made by majority unless the rules require unanimity. (At present, trust law is the opposite of this.)

10. The scheme administrator should be required to file, with the Regulator, an audited statement that contributions have been received at the due time and invested in a timely way.

11. The detailed statutory rules for investment should be replaced with widely defined flexible guidelines, governed overall by a 'statutory prudent investment standard'.

The Regulator should lay down a code of practice for trustees in relation to investment matters. Deviations from the code without good reason should result in intervention by the Regulator in the management of the scheme.

12. Actuaries and scheme auditors should have a duty to report serious or persistent irregularities to the Regulator and, if they do so in good

faith, should be exempt from any legal liability they might otherwise incur.

13. Changes are recommended to the disclosure requirements. In addition, schemes should be encouraged to update and consolidate their trust deeds and rules at least every five years.

14. A compensation scheme should be established to protect scheme members against the default (limited to fraud, theft and other misappropriation) of those dealing with funds' assets.

    An independent Pension Compensation Board should be established. This board would have the sole right to decide whether the compensation scheme should be triggered in any particular case.

    The costs of the scheme should be imposed on schemes generally by means of a levy in proportion to the value of the liabilities which each scheme is required to fund for the purpose of the minimum solvency requirements. No levy would be made unless and until there is an incidence of default.

15. All schemes of more than fifty members should be required to establish a formal internal disputes procedure.

16. The Occupational Pensions Advisory Service (OPAS) should employ paid conciliation staff. The Ombudsman's jurisdiction should be extended to include disputes between the employer and the trustees or among trustees themselves, and he should be given power to enforce his decisions directly.

17. Urgent attention should be given to ways in which pension fund litigation could be expedited, the cost reduced and the position of individual litigants improved substantially.

18. Further work on the division of pension rights in the event of divorce should be undertaken following the Pensions Management Institute Working Group's report.

19. The current basis of tax approval for schemes is extremely complex. There should be a speedy transition to the position where every scheme member is covered by the 1989 Finance Act regime.

    Limited transitional arrangements are recommended to reduce the worst detrimental effects on accrued benefits for existing members.

20. There should be a single Pensions Act to bring the Report's recommendations into effect. It should concentrate on principles rather than detailed regulations, which would, no doubt, follow. Breaches of duty should carry an appropriate sanction. Some should be treated as criminal offences.

12.4.1 The impact of the Goode Committee

The Committee's brief was very wide and the time allowed for its consideration relatively short. Many of the recommendations cover areas in which most UK pension schemes operate in a satisfactory manner. Given that the main impetus for the Committee's establishment was the Maxwell affair, it is considered disappointing by many that its recommendations largely cover areas which are already substantially sound, and are less than rigorous where they deal with matters of real concern. For example, given that it is established that most companies know their contractual obligations – including the provision of defined retirement benefits – the imposition of member-appointed trustees may seem unnecessary. On the other hand, placing the responsibility for anticipating future 'Maxwells' on lay trustees and their advisers might be dismissed as a triumph of hope over experience.

The report is sound, well thought out and comprehensive in relation to the issues as seen by the 'closed system' of UK occupational pension provision. It does not, however, anticipate developments in the social sphere or in government position. It may therefore be 'frozen' in a time and structure of defined benefit pension provision which is already beginning to undergo substantial change.

After the report's publication, the Government responded by issuing seven consultation papers:

1. Introduction and overview.
2. Funding.
3. Scheme management.
4. Early leavers and indexation.
5. Alternatives to guaranteed minimum pensions.
6. Dispute resolution.
7. The regulatory framework.

These were followed by the two-volume White Paper 'Security, equality, choice: the future for pensions'.

12.5 The White Paper

Presented to Parliament in June 1994, the White Paper 'Security, equality, choice: the future for pensions' accepted most of the proposals of the Goode Committee in principle if not in detail. Legislation was promised for the 1994/95 parliamentary session with the majority of changes being made from April 1997.

The main proposals enshrined in legislation are as follows:

1. An Occupational Pensions Regulator will be appointed to focus on schemes which are experiencing difficulties in their funding and operation.
2. Trust law will continue to be the foundation of pension schemes but the government proposes to 'clarify and codify some aspects of trust law and the duties of trustees.'

3. Trustees will be responsible for appointing advisers and in particular the actuary and auditor.
4. Members will have the right to select at least one-third of the trustees with a minimum of two, unless there are fewer than a hundred members when it will be one. This applies to both defined benefit and defined contribution schemes.
5. A formal internal disputes procedure will need to be set up for all schemes as part of the process of resolving members' complaints.
6. Guidelines for the investment of scheme assets will be set, and the trustees will be responsible for the investment policy.
7. A minimum solvency requirement will be introduced following the proposals from the Goode Committee. It will be introduced over a five year period from 1997 with schemes being required to meet the minimum solvency level within the following three years. The minimum solvency position should be checked annually and supported by an actuarial certificate.
8. Actuarial valuations will be required every three years (rather than three and a half years as previously).
9. Information to members must be clearer and timely.
10. Schemes will be encouraged to consolidate their deed and rules at least once every five years.
11. Legislation will be enacted to ensure that in the event of a scheme wind-up each member will actually receive the value of the cash equivalent of their accrued benefits.
12. Transfer value bases must be tightened and the government is looking to the actuarial profession to achieve this and to make allowance for discretionary increases where the granting of such increases has been normal practice.
13. All company sponsored schemes (defined benefit and defined contribution) and personal pension arrangements will be required to provide increases to pensions once in payment at the rate of 5 per cent a year (or in line with prices if less) in respect of the benefits earned after the effective date (suggested as 6 April 1997).

    There will, however, no longer be a requirement to use surplus to increase pensions based on past service unless some of that surplus is to be refunded to the company.
14. Companies will continue to be free to change benefit levels and cease contributions (and thereby wind-up the scheme) but will not be able to reduce accrued rights.
15. A compensation scheme will be established.
16. The actuary and auditor will have a whistle-blowing role requiring them to notify the Regulator in the event of serious breaches of law.
17. Trustees will be encouraged to follow formal procedures in running

their schemes; in particular they will be required to hold at least one formal meeting per year.

18. A new system for contracting-out of SERPS will be introduced in 1997 although the existing system of GMPs and protected rights will continue in respect of service up to then. This will solve some, but not all, of the sex equality problems associated with contracting-out.

19. Separate age-related national insurance rebates will be introduced for contracted-out personal pension arrangements and occupational schemes.

20. Greater flexibility will be given in purchasing annuities from the proceeds of personal pension arrangements enabling the pension to be deferred to age 75 and the opportunity to draw sums from their fund before annuity purchase.

These proposals go much further than simply providing greater security in an attempt to avoid another Maxwell scandal. The Government is continuing the underlying trend of reducing dependency on the state and encouraging individual provision by including greater flexibility for personal pension arrangements.

Companies clearly need to review how their present schemes operate and the impact that these proposals will have. How will member trustees be elected? What should the disputes procedure be? Will it continue to be financially advantageous to contract-out? Will there be another layer of contracting-out bureaucracy? What are the funding and investing implications of minimum solvency? Of compulsory pension increases? Of tightened transfer value bases?

The Pensions Act leaves many questions to be answered in subsequent regulations. Delaying consideration of the issues and principles involved until all the minutiae have been settled can, however, prove to be misguided and expensive in the long run.

12.6 The 1995 Pensions Act

At the time of writing the 1995 Pensions Act has just received Royal Assent. The Act follows the main recommendations of the White Paper, although, as usual, the details are left to be incorporated into Statutory Regulations before implementation in April 1997. There continues to be strong, healthy debate between Government and Opposition, trade unions, employers and the pensions industry, and it is all too clear that pension provision will continue to be a major political issue for many years to come.

12.7 Pension rights on divorce

Traditionally, the value of a divorced spouse's rights to a share of the pension scheme member's benefits were assessed actuarially – if taken into account at all – and added to the lump sum settlement on divorce. In recent times this has been shown to be an unsatisfactory state of affairs, for obvious reasons. Scottish law is better placed to deal with the value of pension rights. They are specifically included in the parties' estates but there is still no statutory guidance on how pension rights should be valued.

In the summer of 1993, the Pensions Management Institute (PMI) in agreement with the Law Society produced a report which is clearly influential and may well form the basis of future law:

1. The PMI report favours the 'clean break' approach; that is, the non-member spouses should be given a once-and-for-all legal entitlement to their own deferred pension from the scheme.
2. The pension should be calculated wherever possible on the statutory cash equivalent basis.
3. The members' own pensions should be reduced accordingly to fund the new spouses' pensions.
4. The 'reasonable' administration costs involved would be borne by the divorcing parties themselves.
5. The newly created pension entitlement would be provided either through the scheme, or by transfer to a separate arrangement.

These would apply equally to England and Wales, and to Scotland. However, the report recognises that any resulting legislation should be framed separately for Scotland, to fit the existing different legal rules there.

The recommendations appear to represent a sensible workable package. It is not clear how a final salary scheme would deal with the member's residual rights, however, and there is the strong legal implication that not only divorced spouses but continuing spouses will effectively be 'members' in their own right. However, in the 1995 Pensions Act the Government continues to prefer the deferred maintenance order approach.

12.8 The Government's agenda

Since the mid-1980s the Government has been conscious of the pressures on state expenditure resulting from an 'ageing population' and changing social and working patterns. Increases in the non-working population, particularly the elderly, will involve an increase in the demand for income and services through the Welfare State structures in the following broad areas:

1. Sickness benefits, medical treatment and medicines.
2. Unemployment and redundancy support.
3. Retirement income.
4. Long-term care.

Underlying the Government's expenditure fears are a high unemployment base and a demographic change from nearly three workers to every pensioner now to two workers to every pensioner in thirty years' time. The real demographic 'timebomb' does not go off until 2010 when the post-war 'baby-boomers' begin to retire but, even so, the existing retired population is growing steadily while becoming older and more in need of care.

The demographic change since the war has been encouraged because of average economic growth rate of more than 3 per cent a year. Such a rate of growth (and possibly 4 per cent a year) is required to support the next bout of changes without lowering living standards. Concern that this is unattainable is perhaps at the core of the Government's thinking.

As indicators of what may happen next to state pensions, sickness and unemployment benefits are already being changed – to taxable incapacity payments (for which the recipient must 'qualify') and a 'job-seeker's allowance'. Senior government spokespersons are increasingly on record as suggesting that social security payments, including pensions, are grabbing an unsustainable share of national income and may have to be cut. This is a European dilemma and other countries are conscious of the problems and are now giving consideration to remedies likely to be required.

12.8.1 Possible pension changes: SERPS

SERPS was introduced in 1978. It was broadly intended to produce pensions of 25 per cent of average 'real' earnings in excess of the basic state pension level (with a maximum). It survived for only ten years before being changed quite radically. In 1988 the target was reduced to 20 per cent of average real earnings and the benefits further worsened by extending the averaging to all of working life rather than the best twenty years. Additionally, the 'contracted-out' personal pension was introduced, with incentives to contract-out of SERPS, and the proportion of the working population not participating in SERPS increased from roughly 60 to 80 per cent. The majority of those now participating are over 45 – ages at which SERPS is good value.

SERPS will undergo further dramatic change and the 1995 Pensions Act proposals for contracting-out herald this. Part of the problem to be solved is the complication resulting from sex equality, where different retirement ages (and therefore accruals), preservation regulations and 'anti-franking' rules present huge problems. Legislation appears likely to simplify contracting-out for future service, but we are left with ongoing complexities of the past.

12.8.2 Possible pensions changes: basic state pension

The basic state pension (the old age pension) is paid to all retired people with a full record of NI contributions. It currently stands at about 20 per cent of national average earnings. After allowing for the married couple's level, it costs over 7 per cent of the incomes of all working people. There is no 'fund' from which to provide it, so those in work are paying for the pensions of their parents and grandparents.

Over the next thirty years, this level of cost can only be sustained if the old age pension increases in line with prices – not in line with earnings generally, so that retired people will be further disadvantaged relative to those in work. Fully linked to average earnings, the old age pension would be expected to cost over 10 per cent of total workforce earnings by 2025. If the state basic pension does only increase in line with prices, it may be expected to fall from 20 to only 11 per cent of national average earnings over the same period.

The Government is faced with a long-term dilemma because the taxation required to continue a universal basic pension at its current real value may be unacceptable. Private pension provision has increased and continues to increase as people retire from maturing company schemes. This will no doubt ameliorate the overall effect and substantially reduce the number of people relying only on the state for retirement income.

It is therefore argued that qualification for the state pension should be tightened towards a form of means-testing, and/or that individuals with good occupational provision should be able to 'opt out' of the state basic pension and the corresponding part of the NI contribution. Furthermore the National Association of Pension Funds (NAPF) has suggested that payment of the state basic pension should be restricted to cases of greatest need.

With a continuing Conservative administration it would be reasonable to expect a contraction in the universal provision of state retirement benefits. Even a Labour government may, despite fundamental support for the Welfare State structure, be tempted to seek ways of encouraging opting out by those who are otherwise well catered for. It would not be difficult to devise a method by which this can be achieved; the only problem for any complexion of government would be the 'phasing-in' arrangements.

12.8.3 Taxation

Approved pension funds benefit from a number of tax reliefs:

1. Employers' contributions are relieved of corporation tax.
2. Employees' contributions are relieved of income tax (but pensions are taxed as income).
3. Dividends and interest are mostly received gross.
4. Capital gains by the fund are exempt.
5. Retirement cash is payable tax-free.

Until a few years ago it was generally felt that these reliefs were inviolable. Then came the earnings cap on pension benefits and tax-relieved contributions, stricter limits on maximum retirement lump sums and changes to advanced corporation tax which means funds cannot reclaim the full tax deducted from dividends.

In changing the tax position of pension funds, the main 'target area' identified is the lump sum, the only fully tax-free benefit. The difficulty of changing expectations would suggest that taxation could only be phased in slowly, perhaps by imposing an overall monetary ceiling or by imposing a very small tax level which increases over a period. It would appear easier to restrict further the ability of funds to reclaim the tax deduction from dividends, but this would reduce the attraction of investment by funds in ordinary shares and, probably, affect the stock market – presumably undesirably.

Another target might be relief on contributions. It would not be impossible to withdraw some of the relief on employer contributions, but the resulting accounting controls and administration might be prohibitive. In addition, of course, a good many other, arguably less desirable, business expenses are offset from profit before tax is charged. The justification for a tax on employer contributions is therefore poor.

Employee contributions are a 'softer' target. A restriction of relief to the basic tax rate, in line with mortgage interest, would be straightforward. Phasing in of tax, over a period up to a tolerable level (say half of basic rate) would also not be out of the question. It should, however, be remembered that pensions are taxed in the same way as pay – and double taxation would not be acceptable. In addition, employees who accepted pay cuts or took smaller pay rises instead of paying contributions would avoid the tax.

Approved pension schemes are, then, a potential target for the Chancellor and the Inland Revenue. It is not suggested that the tax regime will change, but the possibility should never be ruled out.

12.8.4 Approved benefits

The benefits which can now be provided through an exempt approved pension scheme extend to death benefits (lump sums and dependants' pensions), ill-health pensions and the retirement lump sum, provided these are within certain Inland Revenue limits. The approvable benefits, the limits and the Inland Revenue's supervision of them have developed in a way which only with hindsight can be seen as in any way logical. Other benefits in retirement, such as health care, home help and residential care were seen, at least since the Second World War, as being in the Welfare State's province. A reduction in the scope of care provided by the Welfare State might easily produce pressure for an extension of the kind of benefits which may be funded in a tax-effective and therefore attractive way.

At present, it is possible to fund lump sum retirement benefits through unapproved arrangements, although their use is so far largely restricted to provision for employees who are caught by the earnings cap. However, even with these arrangements, the cash sum 'matures' and is released at a retirement date. Ongoing funding, particularly for groups of investors each of whom may (or may not) need to draw on the fund for financing 'care', is more difficult. Ideally there should be an extension of approvable benefits into such socially desirable areas within a few years. This might well take in invalidity benefits (currently insurable as permanent health insurance) and, possibly, redundancy payments.

However, we do not believe the earnings cap applying to the accrual of any approved benefit will be removed. The principle of a cap is reasonably easy to accept; that those earning, say, five times national average earnings or more should be able to provide for themselves, at least in respect of reasonable income replacement above the cap.

12.9 Conclusion

In the field of pensions and benefit provision there is only one certainty and that is that change is here to stay. In designing and reviewing your company's pension provision, future possible changes can be an opportunity as well as a threat and will be ignored at your peril.

Glossary of terms

Accelerated accrual An accrual rate in a defined benefit scheme in excess of one-sixtieth of pensionable earnings for each year of pensionable service.

Accrual rate The rate at which pension is earned by service in a defined benefit scheme.

Accrued benefits The benefits which a member has accrued under a pension scheme at a given date, calculated either in relation to current earnings or projected earnings. In calculating accrued benefits, allowance can also be made for revaluation of deferred benefits and/or pensions in payment required either by the scheme rules or legislation.

Accrued benefits valuation method An actuarial valuation method in which the scheme liability to pay benefits as at the valuation date is based on: (a) the value of current and deferred pensions (allowing for any future increases where appropriate), or (b) the accrued benefits for active members as at the valuation date.

Accrued rights This term is referred to in the preservation and disclosure regulations and has the same meaning as accrued benefits.

Accrued rights premium (ARP) Where a scheme is contracted-out of SERPS by providing GMP, and subsequently ceases to be contracted-out, an ARP may be paid to the DSS to reinstate members into SERPS. This will remove the liability from the scheme to pay GMP.

Active member A member of a pension scheme accruing benefits in respect of current employment.

Actuarial assumptions   The assumptions used by the scheme actuary in producing an actuarial valuation or other actuarial calculations. These include rates of investment return on the pension fund, rates of inflation, increases in earnings, mortality and morbidity.

Actuarial certificate   A brief statement signed by an actuary showing the results of a specific calculation. Such certificates are required in a variety of circumstances such as confirming to the OPB that the scheme is solvent for the purposes of contracting-out of SERPS and for confirming to the PSO the level of any surplus under the pension fund in accordance with the Income and Corporation Taxes Act 1988.

Actuarial deficiency   Where an actuarial valuation shows an excess of liabilities over assets on the basis of a particular valuation method an actuarial deficiency exists. Such a deficiency must always be studied in the light of the actuarial method and assumptions used in producing the report as these will have considerable impact on the size of deficiency shown (and possibly even the existence of a deficiency).

Actuarial increase   An increase applied to benefits deferred after the NPD based on actuarial calculations.

Actuarial liability   The value of benefits under a pension fund in respect of outgoings payable after the valuation date. This liability will be based on a particular valuation method and assumptions.

Actuarial reduction   A reduction in a member's accrued benefits prior to the NPD calculated to offset increases in the cost of paying those benefits.

Actuarial statement   A requirement of the disclosure regulations, a part of the annual report. In it the actuary confirms, in a prescribed form, the security of members' benefits, both accrued and prospective.

Actuarial surplus The opposite of an actuarial deficiency.

Actuarial valuation report A report produced by an actuary in accordance with guidelines laid down jointly by the Institute and Faculty of Actuaries, at least once every three and a half years in respect of self-administered pension schemes (but at least every three years in the case of small self-administered schemes) using actuarial methods to value the scheme's assets and liabilities at a given date.

Actuarial value of assets The value which the actuary places on the assets of a scheme. This may be market value, discounted value of future receipts or some other value.

Actuary In the United Kingdom this means a Fellow of the Institute of Actuaries or of the Faculty of Actuaries. Individuals with other actuarial qualifications may be approved for the purposes of UK legislation by the Secretary of State.

Actuaries employ a knowledge of financial matters and probability in mathematical models to analyse future events. Their methods and assumptions are controlled by professional standards and guidance notes.

Added years The augmentation of a member's benefits under a defined benefit scheme by the granting of notional additional years of accrual, such accrual being funded by a transfer payment, AVCs by the member or by further employer contribution.

Additional component Sometimes referred to as additional pension, this is the state earnings-related pension which has accrued in respect of an employee's income between the lower and upper earnings limits, and is paid in addition to the state basic pension.

Additional voluntary contributions (AVCs) Contributions paid by a member voluntarily, not forming part of regular ordinary contributions (if any). Such contributions can be used to purchase benefits on a defined contribution or defined benefit basis depending upon the particular pension scheme's arrangements.

Administrator

A person whom the PSO and, in some circumstances, the OPB regard as being responsible for the management of the scheme. This term is also used to describe the clerical workers responsible for the day-to-day administration of the fund which includes the broking of risk benefits, calculation of pension benefits and other routine tasks.

Aggregate method

An actuarial valuation method whereby the present value of all benefits (both for past and future service) is calculated and the value of assets is deducted. The difference is then expressed as a percentage of pensionable payroll by dividing by the present value of total projected earnings over active members' expected working lives.

Annual report

The disclosure regulations require the trustees to produce annually specific financial information in respect of their scheme. The Annual Report must include a copy of the audited accounts and of the latest actuarial statement together with the investment manager's report (if self-administered), the auditor's statement on the accounts and a short report from the trustees providing basic information in relation to the scheme constitution. The report can include additional information if the trustees feel this is helpful. Also some larger schemes issue a simplified report designed to encourage members to read it and understand more about their pension scheme. Even if a simplified report is provided, members still have a legal right to see the full report if they so wish.

Appropriate personal pension scheme (APPS)

Any personal pension arrangement or FSAVC scheme granted an appropriate scheme certificate by the OPB, thus enabling the scheme to be used for the purpose of contracting-out.

Appropriate scheme certificate

The certificate issued by the OPB to an APPS enabling that scheme to be used for the purpose of contracting-out.

Approved scheme

A generic term for an occupational pension scheme approved by the Inland Revenue under Chapter I of Part XIV of the Income and Corporation Taxes Act 1988 or an FSAVC scheme approved under that legislation. The term is also used to describe a PP arrangement approved under Chapter IV of Part XIV of that Act. In the case of occupational schemes the term 'exempt-approved scheme' is sometimes used and is a separate category of approval under that Act. (See also 'Exempt approved scheme'.)

Article 119

Article 119 of the Treaty of Rome provides that men and women are entitled to equal pay for equal work.

Basic pension

This is the single person's flat rate state pension paid to all who have met the minimum NI contribution requirements. Widows, widowers and, in some cases, married women can also claim a state basic pension based on the contribution record of their spouse.

Bridging pension

An additional amount of pension paid from an occupational scheme between a member's date of retirement and later state pension age. Once the member attains state pension age the bridging pension normally ceases and is replaced by the state pension which should be of the same magnitude.

Buy out

This normally refers to the purchase by the trustees of an insurance policy or bond in the name of a member or other beneficiary in lieu of entitlement to benefit from the scheme following the termination of that member's pensionable service. The term is sometimes used to refer to the purchase of an insurance policy in the name of the trustees.

Career average scheme

A defined benefit scheme where the benefit accruing in respect of each year of membership is related to the pensionable earnings for that year.

Cash equivalent

The amount of transfer value to which a member has a legal entitlement under Schedule IA of the Social Security Pensions Act 1975 where pensionable service has ceased and the member has a right to a preserved benefit.

Centralised scheme

A pension scheme operated for the members of several different employers. The term can be used in relation to schemes for both associated and non-associated employers.

Class A (or B or C) members

Terms used in specimen rules issued by the PSO applying to members of occupational schemes who join during specified periods. The periods are as follows:

1. Class A – members of schemes established on or after 14 March 1989 and all new members of existing schemes joining on or after 1 June 1989.
2. Class B – members of schemes established before 14 March 1989 who joined between 17 March 1987 and 31 May 1989.
3. Class C – Members who joined schemes before 17 March 1987.

Transitional arrangements exist to exempt members from being treated under Class A or Class B as appropriate where they fall into these classes due to events such as scheme reorganisations and company takeovers. Class B members have a statutory right and Class C members may (if the rules of the scheme allow) elect to be treated as Class A members, but their earnings will then be subject to the earnings cap.

Closed scheme

A pension scheme which cannot accept new members. Contributions for existing members may continue or stop and benefits may or may not be provided in respect of their future service.

Commingled fund

This term is sometimes used instead of common investment fund or exempt unit trust.

Common investment fund   An arrangement allowing the pooling of assets for two or more pension schemes for investment purposes allowing economies of scale and enhanced returns. Such arrangements generally apply to the schemes of employers in a single corporate group.

Commutation   The exchange of all or part of a pension entitlement under a pension scheme for an immediate cash sum.

Commutation factors   The factors used to calculate the amount of pension which needs to be given up for a particular lump sum benefit.

Compliance audit   An audit carried out to ensure compliance with either the rules and regulations imposed by the Financial Services Act, or compliance with Inland Revenue rules and practices as described in Memorandum 102 issued by the PSO.

Compulsory purchase annuity (CPA)   An annuity which must be purchased by a pension scheme for a member on retirement from service.

Continuation option   A term under a life assurance policy whereby a member ceasing to be eligible for that policy can take out a policy in his or her own name under the same basic terms without undergoing a medical examination. Continuation options have been common in the past under group life assurance arrangements held under occupational pension schemes but such terms are becoming less common, particularly since the advent of AIDS.

Continued rights   A term used by the Inland Revenue in the Practice Notes meaning the rights of scheme members who are not Class A members.

Contracting-out   Use of an occupational scheme, PPA or FSAVC scheme which meets certain statutory requirements policed by the OPB to accrue benefits under that scheme or arrangement in place of benefits under SERPS. Under an occupational scheme a member's NI contributions to the state are reduced and in the case of the other arrangements partially refunded to the administrator of the arrangement.

Contracted-out money purchase scheme (COMPS)

A defined contribution scheme which is contracted-out and provides protected rights. A defined contribution scheme can also be contracted out while providing GMPs, but in that case is not a COMPS and is regarded by the OPB as a contracted-out salary-related scheme.

Contracted-out protected rights premium (COPRP)

A COPRP may be paid by a contracted-out money purchase scheme if that scheme ceases to contract-out, to reinstate the members into SERPS. The premium calculation is based on the protected rights and may not fully reinstate the member's SERPS benefits for the period of contracting out.

Contracted-out rebate

This is the amount by which both the employer's and the employees' NI contributions are reduced in respect of employees who are contracted-out. It is equivalent to the payment made by the DSS and referred to as minimum contributions to a PP arrangement or FSAVC scheme.

Contracted-out salary-related scheme (COSRS)

An occupational pension scheme contracted-out and providing GMPs.

Contracting-out certificate

The certificate issued by the OPB to an occupational pension scheme confirming the Board's agreement to that scheme being used to contract its members out of SERPS. The certificate will confirm the employments covered.

Contribution holiday

A period of temporary suspension of the employer's and/or members' contributions, normally used to reduce an actuarial surplus.

Contributions equivalent premium (CEP)

A state scheme premium which can be paid to reinstate a member into SERPS. It applies where a member with qualifying service of less than two years (this was five years for leavers prior to 6 April 1988) leaves a scheme which was contracted out.

Contributory scheme

A scheme to which active members are required to contribute.

Controlling directors (20 per cent directors)

A company director who, with his associates, owns or controls 20 per cent or more of the ordinary shares of the employing company. Practice Notes IR12 (1991) define controlling directors more fully and describe the special restrictions which apply to their benefits.

Custodian trustee

A trustee appointed solely to hold the assets of the trust. The other trustees are responsible for the management of the trust.

Deferred pensioner

Often referred to as a deferred member, a person entitled to a preserved benefit.

Defined benefit scheme

A scheme which promises a particular level or amount of benefit (usually in relation to salary at or close to retirement). This is often referred to as a final salary scheme, although that is strictly only one type of defined benefit scheme.

Defined contribution scheme

A scheme where the benefits are those which can be provided by the fund produced through contributions which are defined at outset. This is often referred to as a money purchase scheme.

Dependant

A person who is financially dependent on a member or pensioner or who was so dependent at the time of death or retirement of the member/pensioner. The PSO will always accept that a spouse or a child below the age of 18 (or who, if older, is still in full-time educational or vocational training) is a dependant. Other individuals must be able to demonstrate some degree of financial dependency on the member to qualify.

Deposit administration

A group insurance policy or pension scheme under which contributions, net of charges, are accumulated in a single fund to which interest and bonuses are added. The proceeds of the fund are used to provide pensions and other benefits.

Direct investment

The method of investment used by a self-administered scheme whereby specific investments are held in the name of the trustees (or in the name of a separate investment manager) instead of scheme funds being invested in insurance policies.

Disclosure Regulations

Regulations made under the Social Security Pensions Act 1975 whereby certain information must be given either automatically, or on request, to members, their dependants and other legitimately interested parties (such as trade unions where they are empowered to negotiate on pensions).

Discontinuance

Discontinuance of contributions to a pension scheme which will lead to the scheme either winding-up or becoming a frozen scheme.

Discretionary increase

Any increase made to a pension either following a regular review or a one-off decision where that increase has not been promised under the provisions of the scheme but is made on a discretionary basis.

Discretionary scheme

A scheme of which membership is at the discretion of the employer. Benefits under such schemes are often negotiated on an individual basis.

Dynamisation

A general term which is used to describe escalation and indexation of benefits as well as the index linking of earnings for the purposes of calculating final remuneration either for calculating scheme benefits or for the purpose of Inland Revenue limits.

Early leaver

A person who ceases pensionable service under a pension scheme prior to the NPD, other than on death, without receiving an immediate retirement benefit.

Early retirement

The retirement of a member prior to the NPD, and receiving an immediate retirement pension. Benefits may be reduced due to early

	payment and can arise on a voluntary early retirement or on ill-health early retirement.
Earmarked policy	A policy which is earmarked to provide benefits for or in respect of a specific member.
Earnings cap	The maximum amount of earnings on which benefits and contributions can be calculated in respect of Class A members, introduced by the Finance Act 1989. The cap was originally set at £60,000 for the tax year 1989/90. It was expected to increase in line with price inflation (not the higher increases traditionally seen in earnings inflation). The cap was frozen over the fiscal year 1993/94 but the link with price inflation was then restored and the cap raised to £76,800 for 1994/95. The cap also applies to net relevant earnings in respect of members of PP arrangements.
Equal access	Rules introduced in the Social Security Pensions Act 1975 prohibiting discrimination between the sexes over the terms of entry to a pension scheme.
Equivalent pension benefit (EPB)	The benefit which a scheme must pay to an employee who was contracted out of the former graduated pension scheme.
Escalation	Regular increases applied to pensions in payment or preserved benefits. Such increases are usually at a fixed rate or in line with a particular index (often capped to restrict cost).
Exempt approved scheme	An occupational pension scheme (established under irrevocable trust) which is approved by the Inland Revenue under Chapter I Part XIV Income and Corporation Taxes Act 1988, giving rise to tax reliefs specified in that Act. Many of the Inland Revenue's rules regulating such a scheme are discretionary, leading to considerable flexibility (and at times, uncertainty) in their application. This contrasts with an 'approved scheme' approved under the same section of the Act but in respect of which there are no discretionary regulations.

Exempt unit trust	A unitised investment portfolio managed by an investment organisation specifically for investors who are exempt from tax, such as pension schemes and charities.
Expression of wish	(Also sometimes referred to as a nomination). A form which pension scheme members complete to nominate their preferred recipient of any lump sum payable on a member's death. Technically the benefit is paid under a discretionary trust to avoid inheritance tax and so the expression of wish is not binding on the trustees.
External investment manager	An investment manager who is not employed solely either by the trustees or the employer.
Final remuneration	The term used by the PSO for the maximum amount of earnings which can be used for calculating maximum approvable benefits. The precise definition is contained in the Practice Notes.
Final salary scheme	Strictly, a type of defined benefits scheme where benefits are calculated by reference to remuneration received shortly before employment ceases. However, it is often used as an alternative term to defined benefits scheme.
Fixed rate revaluation	The fixed rate of increase applied to the GMP of an early leaver for the period from date of leaving to state pension age – currently 7 per cent per annum (see also Limited rate revaluation and Section 21 Orders).
Franking	The practice of using the excess of the normal scheme pension over the GMP at the date of leaving to provide the GMP revaluation. This is no longer permitted.
Free-standing additional voluntary contributions (FSAVCs)	Contributions payable to a separate pension contract effected personally by an active member of an occupational pension scheme. Benefits are secured on a money purchase basis with (usually an insurance company) by contributions from the member only.

Frozen benefit

A preserved benefit which is not subject to revaluation.

Frozen scheme

A closed scheme under which no further contributions are payable but from which members and/or their dependants are entitled to preserved benefits.

Fully insured scheme

A scheme under which all contributions have been invested in an insurance contract which guarantees benefits corresponding to those promised under the scheme rules. This is not the same as an insured scheme where an insurance policy is the only long-term fund investment.

Funding level

The ratio of the actuarial value of the assets to the actuarial value of the accrued liabilities in an ongoing scheme.

Goode Committee

More correctly, the Pensions Law Reform Committee. This was established in 1992 as the Government's response to the losses incurred by the pension schemes of the business empire of the late publishing tycoon Robert Maxwell.

The Committee reported in September 1993 with 218 recommendations. The Government followed this with a White Paper in June 1994 proposing a number of new legislative and other provisions.

Graduated pension scheme

A state earnings-related scheme which commenced on 3 April 1961 and terminated on 5 April 1975.

Group personal pension scheme

An arrangement between an employer and one or more selected providers whereby employees can effect individual PPs on a 'group basis' giving the members preferential terms. Each individual contract remains between the member and pension provider concerned.

Group policy

An insurance policy held to provide benefits in respect of more than one individual.

Guaranteed annuity option

An insurance policy term whereby an annuity can be bought at a guaranteed rate when a member reaches retirement.

Guaranteed minimum pension (GMP)	The minimum pension which a contracted-out salary related scheme must provide as an alternative to the member's SERPS benefit. All employees contracted-out of SERPS whether by GMP or by protected rights will have an amount equivalent to their GMP (or, in the case of protected rights, their notional GMP) deducted from their SERPS benefits.
Hybrid scheme	A scheme where the benefits are calculated on more than one basis, and that which produces the higher amount at the appropriate date is the one which determines the benefits actually payable in respect of an individual.
Ill-health early retirement	Retirement, with a pension, on medical grounds, prior to the NPD. The benefits payable in these circumstances are often higher than those payable under normal early retirement.
Individual arrangement	Normally used to describe an insured arrangement applicable to one member documented by an exchange of letters. This is normally a written agreement between the employer and the member which also defines the terms of the individual arrangement and establishes a trust so that the arrangement can be an exempt approved scheme.
Industry-wide scheme	This is a centralised scheme for non-associated employers. Such schemes are often set up for employers in a particular industry.
Integration	The design of a pension scheme where the benefits take into account all or part of the state scheme which the member will or may be eligible to receive. A common form of integration involves the deduction of an amount equivalent to the state basic pension from pensionable earnings.
Late retirement	Retirement of a member with a pension at a date after the NPD. The pension payable will normally be increased, often actuarially, but sometimes by the counting of the extra years' service as pensionable.

Level annual premium method

A method of determining premium levels to insurance contracts whereby the level remains constant over the working lifetime of the member provided other circumstances remain unchanged.

Limited price indexation (LPI)

Increases payable under Social Security Act 1990 to pensions in payment in excess of any GMP under a final salary scheme equal to 5 per cent a year or the increase in the RPI if less. The requirement will apply automatically to pensions accrued after the appointed day; under the 1995 Pensions Act the date will be April 1997. LPI increases must be provided on all accrued pensions before any surplus funds can be returned from a scheme to the employer.

Limited rate revaluation

A fixed rate of revaluation of 5 per cent a year applied to the GMP of an early leaver for the period between the date of ceasing to be in contracted-out employment and state pension age. A limited revaluation premium must also be paid to the state scheme.

Limited revaluation premium (LRP)

A state scheme premium which is payable in respect of a member who ceases to be in contracted-out employment accruing a GMP. In return for payment of the premium any subsequent revaluation of the GMP up to state pension age above a given level (currently 5 per cent a year) is provided by the state scheme rather than by the occupational scheme. This is one of the alternatives to a Section 21 Order.

Linked qualifying service

Service in a previous scheme in respect of which a transfer payment has been made to the current scheme and which counts as a qualifying service for the purposes of the current scheme.

Lower earnings limit (LEL)

The annual earnings which an employee can receive before Class 1 NI contributions become payable. It is approximately equal to the basic pension.

Managed fund

An investment contract by which insurance companies can offer participation in one or more pooled funds. Such funds are unitised (in the same way as exempt unit trusts) and so the term is sometimes applied to unitised portfolios set up by external investment managers on the trustees' behalf.

Minimum contributions

The contributions payable to a PP arrangement/FSAVC scheme by the DSS in respect of a member who has contracted-out using that arrangement or scheme. The contribution is equal to the partial rebate of NI contributions together with any additional incentive payments which may be payable to encourage contracting-out. The term minimum contributions is occasionally used to describe the basic ordinary contribution paid by a member of a contributory scheme.

Minimum payment

This is the minimum payment which an employer must pay into a contracted-out money purchase scheme and is equal to the reduction in the NI contributions which applies in respect of employees who are contracted-out.

Money purchase

Benefits payable to the member which are equal in value to the contributions paid in respect of that member, usually together with investment return thereon – often referred to as 'defined contribution'.

Money purchase underpin

A minimum benefit guarantee under a defined benefit scheme which is calculated on a money purchase basis.

Net relevant earnings

Earnings from non-pensionable employment or self-employment (after deduction of losses and some business charges on income) used in calculating the maximum contributions payable to an RAC or PP arrangement. The maximum contribution will qualify for tax relief.

From the tax year 1989/90 net relevant earnings have been restricted by the earnings cap.

Normal pension date (NPD)

The date at which a member is entitled to retire with a pension under the rules of a pension scheme. Other terms such as normal pension age, normal retirement age and normal retirement date are frequently used to describe the same date/age.

Occupational Pensions Advisory Service (OPAS)

A voluntary body funded by the DSS set up to provide free help and advice to members of occupational pension schemes and personal pension schemes concerning their rights and obligations. This service is independent of any government bodies or companies from within the pensions industry. The address is: 11 Belgrave Road, London SW1V 1RB.

Occupational Pensions Board (OPB)

This is a statutory body which was set up under the Social Security Act 1973 with functions derived both from that Act and the Social Security Pensions Act 1975. The OPB issues contracting-out certificates and appropriate scheme certificates for schemes which meet the statutory requirements for contracting-out. The OPB also supervises such schemes to ensure that the statutory requirements continue to be met. In addition to this, the OPB ensures that equal access and preservation requirements are satisfied. The Board has also been appointed as the Registrar of Occupational and Personal Pension Schemes and has wide powers to modify scheme rules where those rules fail to allow the scheme to maintain approval or its contracted-out status.

The Board is also required to report to the Secretary of State when requested to do so on matters affecting aspects of occupational pension schemes. The address is: PO Box 2EE, Newcastle-upon-Tyne NE99 2EE.

Open market option

The option under an insurance policy to apply the proceeds to buy an annuity from any insurer rather than solely the one issuing that policy.

Opting out

The statutory right (from 6 April 1988 under the Social Security Act 1986) of an employee to leave or not to join an occupational scheme of the employer.

Pension guarantee

A provision relating to a pension in payment whereby should the member die within the guarantee period a lump sum shall become payable equal to the remaining instalments of pension which would have been paid (or the actuarial value of those payments which will be less) or the pension will continue to be paid for the guarantee period. The guarantee period can be up to ten years, but the lump sum option is not available in respect of a guarantee period longer than five years.

Pension mortgage

A mortgage to be redeemed by the borrower's tax-free cash sum from the pension scheme at retirement. There must be no direct link between the loan and the anticipated cash sum as the pension would cease to be approvable by the Inland Revenue under such circumstances.

Pension Schemes Office (PSO)

The office of the Inland Revenue which grants approval of pension schemes under the relevant tax legislation and monitors their continued compliance with the appropriate tax regulations. The office was known as the Superannuation Funds Office (SFO) prior to 1 April 1992.

The Office is moving premises from Thames Ditton to Nottingham and so currently has two addresses: Lynwood Road, Thames Ditton, Surrey KT7 ODP, and St Nicholas Court, Castle Gate, Nottingham NG1 7AR.

Pensionable earnings

The earnings upon which either benefits or contributions are calculated.

Pensionable service

The service taken into account when calculating benefits under a defined benefit scheme.

Pensioneer trustee

An individual or company with wide experience of pension schemes and dealing with the PSO with particular reference to SSASs. It is a requirement of approval of an SSAS that it has a trustee who is a pensioneer trustee. The individual or company must be registered with the PSO to act as a pensioneer trustee.

Pensioner's rights premium (PRP)

A state scheme premium which is payable in respect of a member or pensioner who is over state pensionable age when a defined benefit scheme ceases to be contracted-out. In return the state scheme will take over the payment of the member's GMP.

Pensions ombudsman

An impartial adjudicator given power to make legally binding decisions on pension complaints from the public. The post was created under the Social Security Act 1990 and the service provided by the Ombudsman is free. The address is currently: 11 Belgrave Road, London SW1V 1RB.

Permanent health insurance (PHI)

Also referred to as prolonged disability insurance. This is an insurance policy unconnected with the pension scheme which provides income during prolonged periods of sickness or disability up to retirement. There is normally a waiting period before payment begins and once in payment the policy may meet the cost of pension scheme contributions as well as paying income for the member.

Personal pension (PP) arrangements

Arrangements approved under Chapter IV of Part XIV of the Income and Corporate Taxes Act 1988, which can be taken out by individuals who are self-employed or in employment which is non-pensionable. Membership is not open to members of occupational pension schemes although such members have the right to opt-out and effect a PP instead. Personal pensions are set up and administered by approved providers, who can be insurance companies, banks, building societies or other selected financial institutions.

Post-89 regime

The Inland Revenue limits which apply to Class A members.

Practice notes (PN)

This sizeable booklet, coded IR12 (1991), describes the main features of the PSO's discretionary practice in respect of exempt approved schemes. The 1991 version only applies to schemes approved from 1 November 1991. The previous version, IR12 (1979), continues to apply to schemes approved prior to that date.

Pre-1 June 1989 continued rights
The rights of a Class B member under an occupational pension scheme.

Pre-17 March 1987 continued rights
The rights of a Class C member under an occupational pension scheme.

Preservation
The requirements prescribing the minimum benefits to be provided under a scheme or arrangement for a member who leaves prior to the NPD. These are specified in the Social Security Act 1973 and various regulations made under it.

Preserved benefits
The benefits accrued in respect of an individual who has ceased pensionable service in respect of whom no transfer payment has been paid. Payment of preserved benefits is deferred until the member eventually retires.

Priority liabilities
Those liabilities which are met as a first call on a scheme's assets upon its winding-up. Schemes usually contain a priorities rule detailing the order in which liabilities are to be met. In addition in respect of contracted-out salary-related schemes specific priorities must be included, giving a high priority to GMPs and some other liabilities connected with contracting-out.

Protected rights
Benefits under an appropriate personal pension scheme or a contracted-out money purchase scheme derived specifically from the minimum contributions/minimum payments as appropriate.

Protected rights annuity
The annuity purchased from an insurance company or friendly society using the protected rights under an appropriate personal pension scheme or contracted-out money purchase scheme.

Qualifying service

The service which qualifies a member for a short service benefit. Currently a member must qualify for a short service benefit after having completed at least two years' qualifying service.

Register

The Register of Occupational and Personal Pension Schemes (currently maintained by the Occupational Pensions Board under the Social Security Act 1990 and regulations thereunder) records all active and paid-up occupational pension schemes and personal pension arrangements as well as FSAVC schemes, unfunded schemes and overseas schemes.

Registered schemes, with the exception of paid-up and frozen schemes, are required to pay a levy which goes towards the upkeep of the Register and also provides funds for the Pensions Ombudsman and OPAS.

Retained benefits

Benefits on retirement or death held in respect of an employee under a scheme relating to an earlier period of employment or self-employment. Inland Revenue limits contained in the Practice Notes sometimes require retained benefits to be taken into account when calculating the maximum benefits payable to a scheme member.

Retirement annuity contracts (RACs)

An annuity contract made between a self-employed person or person in non-pensionable employment and an insurance company or friendly society. Such arrangements existed prior to the introduction of personal pensions (i.e. before 1 July 1988) and are approved under Chapter III of Part XIV Income and Corporation Taxes Act 1988. Since July 1988 no new RACs can be commenced, although contributions can continue to be made to existing contracts.

Revaluation

The increasing of benefits either preserved or in payment.

Revenue undertaking

A standard form of undertaking to the Inland Revenue signed by the scheme administrator agreeing to notify the Inland Revenue of the occurrence of any specified events.

Salary sacrifice

A legally binding agreement which must be in writing between the employer and employee whereby the employee foregoes part of his or her earnings (in a manner which removes all legal ownership of those earnings) in return for which the employer pays a corresponding amount to a pension scheme.

Section 21 Orders

Issued in accordance with Section 21 of the Social Security Pensions Act 1975, these orders specify the rates of increase to be applied to the earnings factors on which both GMPs and SERPS pensions are based. The revaluation is based on the increase in national average earnings.

Section 32 Policy

This term refers to Section 32 of the Finance Act 1981 (now contained in Section 591 of the Income and Corporation Taxes Act 1988) under which a member may transfer his or her accrued pension benefits under a scheme by effecting an insurance policy. The term is now out of date and such a policy is more commonly referred to as a 'buy-out' policy.

Section 49 Scheme

An occupational scheme which was formerly contracted-out which still holds GMPs in respect of members' past service and is therefore still supervised by the OPB under Section 49 of the Social Security Pensions Act 1975 (now Section 53 of the Pension Schemes Act 1993).

Section 226 Annuity

Another term for an RAC.

Segregated fund

A separate portfolio managed by an investment manager on behalf of a pension fund with its own specific investment strategy. It is sometimes used to refer to an individual portfolio of stocks and shares as opposed to a pooled fund.

Self-administered personal pension

A particular type of PP arrangement which allows direct investment in assets other than the usual insurance policies and unitised funds.

Self-administered scheme

A scheme where the assets are invested in media other than insurance contracts. The investment manager may be external or employed by the trustees/sponsoring employer.

Paradoxically, the term does not refer to the method of administering contributions and benefits.

Self-invested personal pension (SIPP)

This is another term for a self-administered personal pension arrangement.

Self-investment

This term is usually understood to mean the investment of a scheme's assets in the sponsoring employer and associated companies. Under the Social Security Act 1990 a limit of 5 per cent was imposed on such investments, with limited exceptions. The self-investment regulations relating to SSASs are less restrictive.

The OPB requires disclosure of certain levels of self-investment as part of its ongoing monitoring of contracted-out schemes.

Short service benefit (SSB)

The benefit to which an early leaver is entitled under the preservation requirements of the Social Security Act 1973.

Small self-administered scheme (SSAS)

A self-administered pension scheme generally with fewer than twelve members, all, or the majority, of whom are usually owners and/or managers of the sponsoring employer.

Solvency ratio

The ratio of the cash value of assets to the actuarial value of the accrued liabilities (on a current cost basis) of a pension scheme assuming it is wound-up at the date of calculation.

State earnings-related pension scheme (SERPS)

The state scheme which provides an additional pension (on an earnings-related basis) to the basic pension.

State pension age

The date from which state pensions are normally payable. These are currently the 65th birthday of a man and the 60th birthday of a woman, but will gradually be changed to the 65th birthday for both sexes by 2020.

State scheme premium

A premium payable to the state from a contracted-out scheme under various circumstances. The basic premiums are: accrued rights premium; contracted-out protected rights premium; contributions equivalent premium; limited revaluation premium; pensioner's rights premium; personal pension protected rights premium and transfer premium.

Statement of recommended Practice 1 (SORP1)

This was issued in 1986 by the Accounting Standards Committee to provide current best accounting practice for pension schemes. Many of its recommendations were included in the Disclosure Regulations.

Statement of Standard Accounting Practice 24 (SSAP24)

The accounting standard detailing how pension scheme costs should be accounted for in the financial statements of the sponsoring employer. SSAP24 requires pension costs to be spread over the working lifetime of members with any payments above or below this amount being shown as pre-payments or under-payments in the company's financial statements.

Statutory discharge

The discharge provided to trustees when a member exercises the statutory right to a cash equivalent under the Social Security Pensions Act 1975 and so takes a transfer payment.

Transfer payment

The securing of a member's benefits once that member has ceased pensionable service through the payment to another pension scheme, to an insurance company to purchase a buy out policy or to a personal pension arrangement.

Trivial pension

The pension under an occupational scheme which is considered so small by the PSO that it can be commuted in its entirety for a lump sum. The current level of pension considered trivial is £260. The exercise of this PSO concession is also governed by preservation and contracting-out requirements.

Unapproved scheme

Under the Finance Act 1989 employers can provide pension benefits under non-approved (commonly referred to as un-approved) schemes. Such schemes can be funded or unfunded and allow employers to provide pension benefits in respect of earnings in excess of the earnings cap. Such schemes do not, however, qualify for tax reliefs available to approved pension schemes although contributions/benefits payable by the employer can be treated as a business expense.

Unfunded scheme

A pension scheme which exists as a promise to the member by the employer but for which no prior funding is made. The employer must, however, account for the accruing cost of the pension in its financial statement in accordance with SSAP24.

Upper earnings limit (UEL)

The maximum level of earnings in respect of which a member pays Class 1 NI contributions.

Valuation date

The effective date of an actuarial valuation or valuation of the scheme's investments.

Vested rights

These are benefits which a pension scheme member has already accrued and are equal to pensions payable to a pensioner, the preserved benefit held in respect of a deferred member and the leaving service benefit which would apply to an active member if he or she ceased pensionable service on the day of calculation.

Waiting period

A period of employment specified in the pension scheme rules which must be completed before an employee is eligible to join the pension scheme for all or some of its benefits. It is quite common for the waiting period to be removed for death benefits. Also the waiting period is sometimes retrospectively counted as pensionable service once the member joins the pension scheme.

Waiver of premium option   A policy term under some personal pension arrangements and RACs whereby the pension provider undertakes to credit regular premiums to the individual's contract if the individual becomes unable to contribute due to a lack of earnings caused by incapacity.

Widow's/widower's guaranteed minimum pension (WGMP)   The minimum level of pension equal to one-half of the member's GMP which must be provided for the surviving spouse of a member as a condition of contracting-out. Qualifying conditions can attach to this benefit.

Winding-up   The termination of a pension scheme by applying the assets of the scheme to secure members' benefits, either by the purchase of immediate and deferred annuities or by transferring the assets and liabilities to another pension scheme. This process will be carried out in accordance with the priority liabilities contained in the priority rule.

Appendix 1
State pension schemes and contracting-out

A.1.1 State pension scheme

Since April 1978 the state pension scheme has been split into two parts, the state basic pension and the state earnings-related pension scheme (SERPS). The state basic pension is provided for all employees who have an adequate NI contribution record. It provides a pension from state pension age (65th birthday for men, 60th birthday for women) of roughly one-fifth of national average earnings for single employees and about one-third of national average earnings for an employee and spouse.

The current (April 1995) basic state pensions are £58.85 per week for a single person and £94.10 per week for a married couple. There is no facility for opting-out of the basic state pension which is provided on top of any benefits from an occupational or personal pension arrangement.

SERPS was introduced in 1978 to provide pensions on top of the state basic pension. The SERPS entitlement is based on earnings between an LEL (roughly equal to the state basic single pension) and UEL, currently (April 1995) £58 per week and £440 per week respectively. These relevant earnings are revalued each year for the purposes of SERPS in line with increases in national average earnings.

The current SERPS pension for people who reach state pension age before April 2000 is one-eightieth of the revalued relevant earnings for each year of relevant employment from 1978. This is subject to a maximum of 25 per cent of the *best* twenty years' revalued relevant earnings for twenty or more years' employment. For anyone retiring from April 2000 onwards, this percentage is being reduced by April 2010 to a maximum of 20 per cent of *average* revalued earnings over the whole of an employee's working life.

The SERPS pension for employment from April 1988 carries a 50 per cent spouse's pension on death after retirement. SERPS pensions increase in line with prices.

A.1.1.1 National Insurance contributions

For the 1995/96 tax year, employees in SERPS pay NI contributions of 10 per cent on earnings between the limits. Employers pay a percentage rate depending on the level of the employee's earnings.

A1.2 Contracting-out

A1.2.1 Salary-related defined benefit schemes

Where a scheme is contracted-out of SERPS it guarantees a minimum level of pension (called guaranteed minimum pensions, GMPs) for members and their spouses in place of SERPS. In return, both the members and the company pay reduced NI contributions.

The minimum pensions which the scheme must provide are the GMP and (where appropriate) spouse's GMP. These are broadly equivalent to the pensions foregone under SERPS, the spouse's GMP being one-half of the member's GMP. The scheme must ensure that the pension the member receives from state pension age is not less than the GMP and that the spouse's pension payable on the member's death is not less than the spouse's GMP.

The scheme must give 3 per cent a year increases in payment to any GMP or spouse's GMP earned from 6 April 1988. The state provides any extra increases needed to ensure that the GMP and spouse's GMP are protected against price inflation.

The NI contributions rebates applying from 1994/95 in return for a scheme taking contracting-out liabilities are as follows:

1. Employees – 1.8 per cent of earnings between the LEL and UEL;
2. Company – 3 per cent of earnings between the LEL and UEL.

These rebates will reduce in future years.

A1.2.2 Defined contribution schemes and personal pension arrangements

That part of the NI contributions which represents the rebate for contracting-out is accumulated separately and is known as protected rights. It is this amount which is treated as the equivalent of the SERPS benefit which has been foregone. The protected rights fund must be used to secure pension at state pension age in a form which is similar to GMPs providing a spouse's pension and increases to pensions once in payment at the rate of 3 per cent a year.

Appendix 2
Inland Revenue limits for tax-approved schemes

A2.1 Occupational pension schemes

The following is a summary of the limits on contributions and benefits applicable to membership of an occupational pension scheme. These are to be found partly in legislation (Income and Corporation Taxes Act 1988 and various finance acts) but are mainly derived from the wide discretion given to the Pension Schemes Office (PSO) to make rules in connection with the granting and maintenance of exempt approval under Chapter I Part XIV of the Income and Corporation Taxes Act 1988.

The PSO in consequence has used its discretion to develop a significant number of rules, many of which are published in its Practice Notes (PN), coded IR12. There are two basic versions of these, first published in 1979 and 1991, both of which have subsequently been updated and amended. The 1991 version automatically applies to all schemes first approved after 29 November 1991, but schemes approved before that date may elect to be subject to some or all of the 1991 PN provisions. However, whichever version of the PN applies it is important to remember that they are only a guide to the way in which the PSO will exercise its considerable discretion, and the items which are omitted can be just as important as those which are included.

The regulatory picture is further complicated by the fact that there are currently three different statutory approval regimes in force (under Finance Act 1989, Finance (No. 2) Act 1987 and Finance Act 1970), and these apply individually to members, depending variously upon the date the scheme was first approved and the date the member first joined it. The situation is extremely complicated therefore and it is neither possible nor desirable to cover it comprehensively in a book of this size. Consequently this is a brief summary of the main limits applicable to members subject to the newest, 1989, regime since over time this will gradually become the regime applicable to most members.

A2.1.1 Definitions

The following terms have the definitions shown below where they are used in this summary.

1. *Earnings cap* – for the tax year 1994/95 it is £76,800.

2. *Final remuneration* – the greater of:
   (a) the highest taxable remuneration for any one of the last five years, comprising basic pay for the year plus the average of any other emoluments over a three or more consecutive years period of which the basic pay year is the last, and
   (b) the yearly average of the total Schedule E taxable emoluments for any three or more consecutive years ending within the last ten years.
   Final remuneration cannot exceed the amount of the earnings cap.   ⋅
3. *Retained benefits* – broadly, benefits built up in previous employments or periods of self-employment.

The maxima shown below apply in aggregate to all schemes of which the individual is a member in respect of any employment. References to service with an employer include service with an associated employer.

A2.1.2 Maximum contributions

1. *Members* – 15 per cent of remuneration in any tax year. AVCs are included in the 15 per cent.
2. *Employers* – no specific limit, just restricted to ensure that benefits will not exceed appropriate limits.

A2.1.3 Pension at retirement

One-thirtieth of final remuneration (up to twenty years) for each year of service with the employer. Where the member has retained benefits, they are added to the pension from the current scheme and the aggregate cannot exceed two-thirds of the member's final remuneration.

A2.1.4 Cash sum at retirement in exchange for pension

Three-eightieths of final remuneration for each year of service (up to forty years). If greater, a lump sum of up to 2.25 times the initial annual rate of pension to be paid to the member (calculated before exchange for cash and any other benefit). The cash sum is paid tax-free.

A2.1.5 Benefits on death in service

A lump sum of the following:

1. The greater of:
   (a) £5,000 and
   (b) four times final remuneration, less any retained benefits
   plus

2. A pension to one or more of the member's spouse and/or dependants. Where there is one person, the limit is two-thirds of the maximum pension which could be paid to the member on retirement. Where there are two or more pensions the aggregate pensions paid cannot exceed the member's maximum permissible pension.
3. A return of member's contributions with interest.

A2.1.6 Benefits on Death after retirement

1. Maintenance of the member's pension for the balance of a guarantee period of up to ten years after retirement (with the option of payment in lump sum form where the guarantee period does not exceed five years), plus
2. A pension to one or more of the member's spouse and/or dependants. Where there is one person, the limit is two thirds of the maximum pension which could have been provided for the deceased member at retirement if they had no retained benefits, increased in proportion to the rise in the RPI between retirement and death. Where there are two or more pensions the aggregate pensions paid cannot exceed the member's maximum permissible pension.

A2.1.7 Benefits on leaving

A deferred pension for the member of the greater of (1) and (2), as follows:

1. One-sixtieth of final remuneration for each year of service (up to forty years).
2. The lesser of:
    (a) one-thirtieth of final remuneration for each year of service (up to twenty years), and
    (b) two-thirds of final remuneration less any retained benefits.

A2.2 Personal pension arrangements

The position in respect of personal pension arrangements is much simpler.

A2.2.1 Maximum contributions

The appropriate percentage of net relevant earnings taken from Table A.1 where net relevant earnings are, broadly, taxable earnings from the trade or employment carried on by the member, not exceeding the earnings cap.

Table A.1

Age on previous 6 April	Percentage of net relevant earnings
35 or less	17.5
36–45	20
46–50	25
51–55	30
56–60	35
61 or more	40

There are no restrictions on the size of the benefits to be paid from the arrangement, except that the maximum tax-free cash is limited, broadly, to 25 per cent of the total fund held.

Index

Reference should also be made to the Glossary

accrual rate 44
actuarial valuation 28
    defined contribution schemes 111–15
    demographic assumptions 112–13
    disclosure of details 85, 87
    financial assumptions 113
    solvency 114
    White Paper proposals 155
actuary
    appointment/selection 27–8, 61
    duties/roles 27, 28, 92, 109–10, 152, 155
additional voluntary contributions (AVCs) 7,
        12–13, 50–1, 80
administration, day-to-day 69–87
    benefits 70–6
        death benefits 75–6
        early leavers 70–1
        pension increases 74–5
        retirement 73–4
        transfers in 72–3
        transfers out 71–2
    checklist 84
    communications *see* separate entry
    contributions 69–70
    record-keeping *see* separate entry
    review 124
administration fees 34
advisers
    choosing 21–38
        actuary 27–8
        auditors 30
        checklist 36
        investment consultant 28–9
        investment managers 30–2
        legal adviser 29–30
        pensions consultant 22–7
        scheme administrator 32–4
        trustees 34–5
    powers and duties 59
Annual Report and accounts, details to be
        disclosed 85, 86
annuities 156
audit 30
    see also review
auditors 30, 103, 152, 155

balance of cost schemes *see* defined benefit
        schemes
bank accounts 79, 102
Barber v *Guardian Royal Exchange Assurance
        Group* 145–6
Beddoes application 107–8
benchmark risk 92
benefits
    administration *see* administration,
        day-to-day
    approved 160–1
    assessment of future 109–10
    impact of salary increases 118–19
    statements 82, 86
Bilka Kaufhaus case 42
Birds Eye Walls v *Roberts* 146
bridging pensions 146
buying out pensions in payment 63

cessation of employer participation 61–2
cessation of scheme 61–2
    see also winding-up
Coloroll 147
communications
    with authorities 81
    Disclosure of Information Regulations 1986
        85–7
    with members 82, 85–7
    review 124–5
    scheme booklet 82, 125
    statement of accrued benefits 82
    summary of details of items to be disclosed
        86–7
    trustees' Annual Report 82–3, 125
commutation of pension 80, 191
compensation scheme 153, 155
computer, records held on 80–1
contributions
    assessment of future 109–10, 111–14
    collection and investment 69–70
    Inland Revenue limits 191–3
    refunds 79
court action 107–8

Data Protection Act 1984 76, 80–1
death
    disclosure of scheme information checklist
        85

death (*continued*)
  payment of lump sum 58, 75
death after retirement 50
  benefits, Inland Revenue limits 192
  benefits administration 75–6
death in service 49–50
  benefits
    administration 75–6
    free cover level operated by insurance
      companies 77–8
    Inland Revenue limits 191–2
  FURBS 140–1
  UURBS 136
Debt on Employer Regulations 150–1
deferred annuities, with-profit 7–8
defined benefit schemes 5–6, 90–1, 109, 123
  design *see* design of scheme
  see also final salary scheme
defined contribution schemes 5, 123
  actuarial valuation 111–15
  contracting-out of SERPS 189
  design 51–2
  financing 111–20
  investment strategy 90
  updating records 78
delegation of duties 60
dependants' pensions 49–50, 75
deposit administration contracts 8
design of scheme 39–53
  allocation of powers 54–6, 60–5
  checklist 53
  defined benefit scheme 41–51
    accrual rate 44
    death after retirement 50
    death in service 49–50
    early retirement 47–8
    eligibility 41–2
    final pensionable salary 45
    leaving service benefits 48–9
    lump sum benefits 46–7
    member contributions 50–1
    normal retirement date 43
    pension increases 45–6
    pensionable salary 44–5
  defined contribution scheme 51–2
  employee profile 40
  flexible benefits 52
  initial considerations 39–41
  pension scheme objective 40
  target retirement income 40–1
  work profile 39
disclosure of information
  checklist 85
  review 124–5
Disclosure of Information Regulations 82,
    85–7, 124
discretionary benefits, award of 62
divorce, pension rights 153, 156–7
documentation, review 125

earnings cap 45, 129–31, 159, 161, 190
  see also unapproved retirement benefits
    schemes
eligibility 41–2
employer contributions, level of 63
European Court 42, 144, 145–6, 148
expression of wish form 77

final pensionable salary, definitions 45
final remuneration, definition 191
final salary scheme 71, 78
  see also defined benefit scheme
finance, review 126
Finance Act 1986, surplus 116
Finance Act 1989, earnings cap 129
financial records 79–80
Financial Services Act 1986 25, 101
financing of scheme
  defined contribution schemes 111–20
  UURBS 136–7
flexible benefits 52
free-standing additional voluntary
    contribution (FSAVC) 7, 13
funding, review 126
funding level 111
funding surplus 115–16

Gerardus Cornelius Ten Oever case 146
Goode Committee 2, 29, 64
  appointment of advisers 32
  appointment of Pensions Regulator 108
  communications and disclosure 83, 124
  compensation scheme 153
  impact of 153–4
  internal disputes procedure 153
  pension rights on divorce 153
  solvency 115, 151
  summary of main recommendations 151–3
  transfer values 152
  trustees 34, 152
Government's agenda 157–61
  approved benefits 160–1
  basic state pension changes 158–9
  SERPS 158
  taxation 159–60
group personal pensions 7, 16

health, evidence of 77–8
hybrid schemes 6

incentive schemes, UURBS 137
increases in pension 45–6, 74–5
individual arrangements 13–14
inflation-proofing 148–50
Inland Revenue
  certificate of solvency 110
  limits for tax-approved schemes 190–3
  records required 79
  see also taxation

insured pension schemes 7–10
  protection of members' interests 99–100
  unitised funds 9–10
  versus self-administered 11–12
internal disputes procedure 153, 155
investment 60, 88–97
  checklist 98
  liability profile of the scheme 92–3
  powers 89
  review 126
  risk 88, 91–2
  strategy 88, 89–91
  vehicles 93
investment advice, authorisation 25
investment consultant, selecting 28–9
investment manager
  appointment and role 88–9
  cost of transferring assets from one manager
      to another 96–7
  fees 32
  manager risk 92
  monitoring performance 96–7
  selection 30–2, 37, 95–6
  standard agreement 31–2
investment manager structure 93–5

late-joining employees 63
leavers' records 79
leaving service
  benefits 48–9, 70–1, 192
  disclosure of scheme information checklist
      85
  FURBS 140
  member with less than two years'
      qualifying service 70–1
  UURBS 135–6
legal adviser, selecting 29–30
liability profile of the scheme 92–3
limited price indexation (LPI) 74–5, 149–50
lump sum benefits 46–7

managed funds 9, 11
managing committee 59
market risk 91

Maxwell affair 99
members
  annual benefit statements 125
  contributions 50–1
  options 63
  records 77
  rights and benefits 58
money, movement from and between outside
      managers 102–3
money purchase schemes see defined
      contribution schemes
money purchase underpin 52

national insurance rebates 156

Neath v *Hugh Steeper Ltd* 46, 146
new employees 61
new members 77, 85
nomination form 77

Occupational Pension Schemes (Disclosure of
      Information) Regulations 30
Occupational Pensions Advisory Service
      (OPAS) 106–7
Occupational Pensions Board 81

part-time employees 42
PAYE tax records 79
payment of scheme expenses 61
payments, tax deducted 79
Pension Schemes Act 1993 144
Pension Schemes Office 81, 190
pensionable salary, definitions 44–5
Pensions Act 1995 103, 156
  appointment of advisers 32
  appointment of Pensions Regulator 108
  limited price indexation (LPI) 150
  solvency 115
  trustees 34
  winding-up surplus 116
pensions administrator, selecting 38
pensions consultant
  attributes required 22–3
  combination of role with actuary 27
  fees/commissions 26–7
  selecting 22–7
Pensions Law Review Committee see Goode
      Committee
Pensions Ombudsman 107
Pensions Regulator 108
personal pension arrangements 7, 14–16
  appropriate arrangements 15
  approved providers 15
  contracting-out of SERPS 189
  group schemes 16
  homes for transfer values 15
  retirement annuity contracts 15–16
pooled funds 93, 99–100
portfolio insurance 94
powers, allocation between trustees and the
      company 54–8, 60–3, 60–5, 66
professional indemnity insurance 25
protection of members' interests 99–108
  insurance policies and pooled funds 99–100
  role of auditor 103
  self investment 103–6
  self-administered schemes 100–6

record-keeping 76–81
  changes in employees' circumstances 77
  Data Protection Act 1984 76, 80–1
  employee who declines to join 76
  leavers' records 79
  medical evidence 77–8

record-keeping (*continued*)
  members' records 77
  pension records 79
  pensions subject to increases 79
  proof of marriage 77
  scheme financial records 79–80
  spouse's date of birth 77
  transfer records 78
  updating records 78
Registrar of Occupational Pension Schemes 81
remedies available to beneficiaries 106–8
  court action 107–8
  Occupational Pensions Advisory Service
    (OPAS) 106–7
  Pensions Ombudsman 107
  Pensions Regulator 108
retained benefits, definition 191
retirement
  early 47–8
    benefits administration 73–4
    due to ill-health 73–4
    FURBS 140
    UURBS 135
  late, benefits administration 74
  normal
    benefits administration 73–4
    date 43
  planning using unapproved schemes 141–2
retirement annuity contracts 15–16
review 121–6
  aim 122
  balance of powers 125
  communications and disclosure 124–5
  documentation 125
  funding, finance and investment 126
  general administration 124
  scheme benefit structure 122–3
  trustees' effectiveness 126
rights and benefits of members 58

salary increases 118–19
salary-related defined benefit schemes,
    contracting-out of SERPS 189
scheme administrator, selecting 32–4
scheme amendments 62
scheme benefit structure, review 122–3
scheme booklet 82, 125
scheme documentation 76, 85, 87
sector risk 91–2
security of scheme assets 99–108
  bank accounts 102
  cash 102
  cheques 102
  insurance policies and pooled funds 99–100
  movement of money from and between
    outside managers 102–3
  role of auditor 103
  self investment 103–6
  self-adminstered schemes 100–6

segregated fund 10, 93, 97
self investment 103–6
self-administered schemes 10–11
  appointment of external custodians 101
  charges 11–12
  portfolio management 101
  protection of members' interests 100–6
  stock lending 102
  use of internal pensions manager 12
  versus insured schemes 11–12
SERPS 158
  contracting-out 16–17, 156, 189
  definition 188
  national insurance contributions 188
settlement of disputes 61
Sex Discrimination Act 1986 144
sex equality 42, 143–8
  case examples 145–7
  costs of 149
  European Court judgments 144, 145–6, 148
  legislation 144
  solutions to equalisation 147–8
small self-administered pension schemes
    (SSAS) 10–11
Smith v *Avdel Systems* 147
Social Security Act 1990
  Debt on Employer Regulations 150–1
  limited price indexation (LPI) 149–50
Social Security Acts 1985 and 1986 117
Social Security Pensions Act 1975 144
solvency 114, 151, 155
solvency certificates 110
specific risk 92
state earnings-related pension scheme *see*
    SERPS
state pension
  contracting-out 188
  possible changes 158–9
  retirement ages for males and
    females 143–4, 148
stock lending arrangements 102
surplus 115–16

tactical asset allocation 94
taxation
  Government's agenda 159–60
  reliefs 159
  see also Inland Revenue
transfer values 15, 62, 85, 117, 152, 155
transfers in 72–3, 78
transfers out 71–2
trust, description 56
Trustee Investment Act 1961 89
trustees
  Annual Report 82–3, 125
    certificate of solvency 110
  appointment 34–5, 60
  the company as 57
  decision-making process 60

trustees (*continued*)
  duties 57–8, 99
  effectiveness, review 126
  Goode Committee recommendations 152
  powers 54–8, 60–3, 60–5
  removal 34, 60
  security of assets 99
  selection, White Paper proposals 155
types of pension scheme 5–18
  see also under individual scheme

unapproved retirement benefits schemes
      17–18, 130, 131–42
  definition 131
  funded (FURBS) 137–41
    advantages and disadvantages 138–9
    common design features 139
    death-in-service 140–1
    definition 137
    early retirement 140
    leaving service 140
    normal retirement 139–40
    why set up under trust 137–8
  retirement planning 141–2
  tax treatment 133 Table
  unfunded schemes (UURBS) 132–7
    advantages and disadvantages 132–4
    death-in-service benefits 136
    early retirement 135

  employee contributions 137
  final salary promise 134
  financing 136–7
  incentive schemes 137
  leaving service 135–6
  money purchase benefits 135
  normal pension age 134
  see also earnings cap
unitised funds 9–10
UURBS, insurance 137

waiting period before joining 41–2
White Paper 'Security, equality, choice: the
      future for pensions'
  actuarial valuations 155
  appointment of advisers 32
  appointment of Pensions Regulator 108
  compensation scheme 155
  contracting-out of SERPS 156
  internal disputes procedure 155
  main proposals 154–6
  national insurance rebates 156
  solvency 115, 155
  trustees 34, 155
widows'/widowers' pensions
  death of member after retirement 50, 73
  death of member in service 49–50
winding-up 55, 85, 116